MONEY MAGIC

THE ALCHEMY OF FINANCIAL FREEDOM

CAT HOWELL

ISBN: 978-1-7386146-0-8

cathowell.com

He who is going to be initiated must pass through the creature to be born a new man.

- De Vries

CONTENTS

PREFACE

Blue velvet sofa, twenty dollars a lap dance, I make a mental bet that the guy will cum in his pants before the song is even over.

There's some rich patrons, they book out the VIP and purchase bottles of Hennessy. The girls pour amaretto over their bodies and lick it off each other.

It's all worth it though, at the end of the night, counting dollar bills from my black leather thigh highs. Everyone knows money comes at a sacrifice, and a pound of flesh seems a fair price.

Besides, if this is what it takes to keep me off the streets, then call me a sinner.

I didn't grow up thinking that I'd end up here. Dancing in dimly lit clubs thick with cigarette smoke.

A bright, and promising young girl, straight A's, always lost in a book. We never had much money growing up, but my parents both worked hard and did what they could. I dreamed of someday becoming a published author.

I was destined to follow the path of good grades > graduate > good job > work hard > retire when I'm older.

Then my sexuality happened, I discovered boys, went wild with a desire to live life on my terms. My dreams of writing quickly pushed to the side.

Now, a highschool dropout, without experience, without connections, lost in a world of drugs and alcohol, what choice was there to make?

The dots blur, each night I'm numbing.

Some shifts I clear $2,000 (but the average is more like $300), despite this I never have anything to show for. It's like I'm a leaky bucket, money seems to come and go.

The golden handcuffs, that's what the girls call it. Once you're in the industry it's hard to get out. The more you hustle, the more you make.

I let myself down, and others mirror this back. Some even break my heart.

Money antagonizes me, but I depend on it.

It is some-thing. What that thing is, I could not tell you. Those with it hold great power and those without it pay the price. A force that is separate to love.

The girls and I joke about being swept off our feet by men who will take care of us financially. This seems like the only realistic way for me to succeed.

In my journal I write "I hate my life".

I lose myself to stay afloat, and everything around me burns to flames.

Then, one night, while I'm trying to convince a patron to part open his wallet, leaning ever so closely so he can see the deep crease of my cleavage, a dragon comes to visit me.

It appears so quickly. Above the stage, a haze of ivy and copper tinted sugar blew. I shook my head and blamed it on the alcohol. But the enchantment never left me.

From that day forth everything changed.

From the ashes I would rise.

Eventually going on to trade the six inch heels for sandals and building three million dollar companies, exiting out of one in 2021, publishing a book, and mentoring others on their own relationship with money.

Throughout the years, I have come to experience almost every flavor of financial relationship there is—from homelessness to financial dependency, to having dependents, to sacrificing myself for cash, making millions, losing it all and rebuilding again.

These days, my relationship with money is in stark contrast to what it once was—it comes through flow, with ease, and without the anchors of sacrifice. It is a relationship that feels deeply safe, loving, and playful.

This is my wish for you.

My intention with Money Magic is to share with you the kind of money story I wish I had been exposed to all those years ago, one that will create a real and measurable shift in your current circumstances.

It is particularly written for the creatives in the house, the visionaries, the entrepreneurs, the artists, and the dreamers.

Inside these pages I will be taking you into an astral plane where a great beast roams, paralleling this with my own story, and a practical guide for you to apply in your own life. And while it may seem childish to think that a tale of a dragon could change your financial circumstances, know that there is nothing more powerful in this world than story.

For it is through the stories we share that we come to forge our beliefs, and therefore our very experience of money.

The narratives we spin, some from our own memories, others borrowed, determine our identities, it is the folklore of our selves. We are fluid: mutable, we transform. The same is true of myth.

I have seen people scale their businesses to million dollar months within a matter of months using the concepts within. Others attract better, higher paying jobs and opportunities. What is more impressive than the numbers, however, is how they are achieving this. In total play, flow and without sacrifice or compromise of their values, selves or wellbeing.

I've seen the impossible happen.

Ride with me, trust me, even when it feels like I'm taking you down a rabbit hole, I promise the dots will connect. Once you start seeing the dragon, you won't be able to unsee it.

Whether you are facing looming debt, plateauing at a certain income level, recovering from past failures, or simply desire to support loved ones or enhance your lifestyle, the principles within will help you to achieve that which you desire.

As you go through this book, take your time to marinate in the concepts, to feel the truth of them in the context of your own life. Ponder the possibilities and play with the ideas.

Take what resonates with you, and pay even closer attention to what irritates or triggers you, these are always portals. And most importantly—integrate. You are the only person here that can guarantee the results.

Trust yourself. Trust the process. And enjoy the encounter with your dragon.

Cat

1

THE GREAT BEAST

There's an astral plane. With two suns in the sky.

Snakes that curl upon themselves, the symbol of infinity. It is a place of transformation and renewal, a land where a great beast roams.

Lavender fields once stretched as far as the eye can see against a mountainscape of jagged white-tips framing the horizon. Dunes of gold that rose and fell, and palms that rubbed against waterfalls.

At night, the lake would burn like a torch, glimmering from the precious gems concealed within.

Petals tumbled down like scented snow, candied fruit, jellies bright as costumed jewels, gilded cups and copper helmets, stranger than a dream.

From a seed that glowed iridescent as the cap of a mushroom, a creature sprang forth.

Imprinting to its Master. A bond that could never be broken, stronger than any mortal connection.

Scales that shone as bright as sapphires. Long, blue, liminal body. Effervescent in the color of octarine.

Flying through the darkness, wrapped in fire, stone-split ruins, windy cliffs, and caves where water poured.

Dragon circled, leaving a trail of silver. Like smoke, gone through the clouds.

A mischievous being, child of the stars, it barked and rejoiced, sending echoes through the land.

From the rocks, and tunnels that ran underground, where mists streamed like purple genies, diamonds spilled forth adorning the trees like delicate bracelets.

These treasures were Master's birthright.

But the land has since changed.

No longer do the rivers flow in honey and gold.

No longer do great treasures spill forth from the earth in abundance.

The flowers have wilted and soured. The dunes of gold have turned to dust.

Master's dreams now taste like metal. Now taste like smoke.

Dragon lumbers, striped neck as if in agony. Scale-studded writhing as a serpent.

Ever since, the great beast has developed a penchant for flames.

Vomiting fire everywhere it goes.

Now, even the sunlight has difficulty navigating its way through the clouds of cinder, coming to the horizon and seemingly stopping short with its finger on its lips.

Dragonflies that once shimmered in emeralds, lay dead across the ground, poised as if to fill the void, wings burned to a crisp.

Sucking, slurping, lips like the inside of a plum. Wet gooseberry skin that folds into talons caked in blood. Steam rising from its snout.

Have mercy, the trees groan. They stand like twisted soldiers, barren of their leaves of jade, sharing sustenance below the ground to their damaged comrades.

The bark crumples and weevils dig.

The dryads lament the ash-colored fields.

The jewels turn to rust and the waterfalls thicken to slush.

Building, oozing, glitching.

A pulse, barely perceptible.

Master's scent is always on the wind. It drives the beast to the brink of wild obsession.

Dragon circles, leaving a trail of lava. Molten hot, just like Master's thoughts.

2

SNAKES

"Like the snakes they would draw on the coffins of the dead." Hands covered in oil, stained in black.

Gee says I'm too impulsive. That I should think things through before acting on them. Perhaps if I did, then I wouldn't be in the mess I'm in.

He's right, of course, but what is done is done, now I just need to deal with the consequences.

"Why does it have its tail in its mouth?" He asks, pointing at the slick strips of clay laid limp on the table.

But I'm a preacher in a fever. My sermon continues with a new topic. "The lines across your neck are all the times you were hung for witchcraft in past lives." I conduct the air towards my own neck, showing him the telltale signs of a witch. I fill his head with wisdom.

"I don't have any lines."

"Then you were the problem."

"I was a turtle."

A mind that flips and flops, he'd once told me, he can't keep up. Nor can I. One minute I'm lost to a million ideas, the next they've withered like a shrunken patch of forest.

Magic, I told him when we'd first met. *How could you not know it?*

That's made up, he'd replied.

Nothing wrong with that, I'd said.

He is a seed of doubt. He believes in magic in the same way he believes in heaven—it doesn't exist. How could I possibly begin to explain such complex things to him?

That it was magic that had kept my feet cool. Nurturing me back to the land of the living.

That it was magic that had connected me into a great tapestry.

It all feels like a lifetime ago.

Where is your magic now? He chides.

It has forsaken me.

I pick one of the clay strips up and push my fingers into the soft form to shape a snake's head. My lips a thin line of misery.

"What's the point of these snakes anyways?" Gee asks.

"They're the symbol of alchemy." I don't think any more about his question. A mind that fills its void with a subterranean world where stardust collides.

Snakes, spray painted second hand mirrors, carved wooden sigils. All in the name of flow. Gee tolerates it, with mild curiosity. I, in turn, tolerate him because it feels good to have someone to confess it to, even with his dubious side-long glances. He's the only one that knows I'm a witch and I intend to keep it so. I'm most certain that to admit to my magical practice publicly would bring me great shame and embarrassment.

I line the oven tray with my clay figurines and put the timer on. Pressing my t-shirt down, removing the creases and pausing to ponder something important to say.

"Do you want to hear what the psychic told me last week?"

"Psychics suck." He says.

"Why?"

"Because they're not real."

"I get premonitions that come true."

"More like you smoke too much weed."

Flush of shame feels so good it's like whiskey to the veins.

"Fine I won't tell you."

"Fine, tell me."

I consider my words. Let it get real quiet to the point where we can hear the lone fly buzzing around the room.

"She said you're the one blocking my money."

He laughs, a laugh black as a raven's, eyes rolling back, he mumbles, 'Blame it all on me'.

I had made millions and now had nothing to show for. Blame it all on you.

"I'm sorry," I say, my words rejected. But he pretends not to hear me and starts scrolling through his phone. There's a post about how detox is better than bulking, someone announcing they are fed up with the weather, an ad promoting five star villas in Thailand, a rant about ai replacing humans, and a friend stating "Project Veritas, you're FIRED!".

The fly bothers him and he stands up to try to swat it, he misses and flicks the window open to swoop it out. Satisfied, he sits once more.

My new business has ground to a halt. All of my creative inspiration and sense of purpose out the door.

No matter how many emails I craft or send out, no matter what I post, no one is biting.

It's just getting worse.

Follow flow, I remind myself. What else am I to do?

Above the mantelpiece is a line of black obsidian mirrors.

There's a reel of two dogs barking at each other across a fence on Gee's phone. He laughs.

The oven timer goes off.

I pull the tray with the little snake figures still steaming with heat.

"Kinda looks like a dragon," he says, peering over my shoulder.

3

THE MYTH OF MONEY

How is myth born?

It is a massing, a collection of ideas and unknowns, flocking and weaving together through a hairline crack of time.

Something so compelling that we are inspired to repeat it. Passed down from person to person, each embellishing the narrative for the next.

For over twenty-seven thousand years, since the first cave paintings were discovered, telling stories has been one of our most fundamental communication methods. Our brains synchronizing to the storyteller's[1].

Each time a story is retold it changes. Glorified, minimized, exaggerated and vilified.

Crafted to answer timeless questions, moral codes, and serve as a compass for the unknown and unexplainable.

Through myth we make sense of our world.

Pandora's box, the boy who cried wolf, the legend of Sleepy Hollow.

And there exist few myths more universal and conflicted than the one of money itself.

Embedded directly into the human experience, we cannot deny our transactional reality. The wifi network we connect to, the food we consume, the doctor visits and clothing we wear. Even the beautiful sunset may have cost a bus ticket or a motel payment to be able to enjoy.

We require money to live and survive, we use money as a form of self expression, to enhance our experiences, yet stutter our way through it sharing stories of sacrifice, suffering, greed and betrayal.

It is a narrative unlike any other, marred in desire, longing, anxiety, frustration and fear.

In its pursuit, wars have been waged, families torn, and murders committed.

Wealth and spiritual growth are perceived as polarizing forces. To be spiritually enlightened is to renounce all material attachment and to martyr oneself to financial destitution.

And such is the juxtaposition humanity finds itself in.

We share tales of the horrors of money, we renounce it in the name of wellbeing, sneer at those who possess it, feel ourselves shackled to a monetary system all the while secretly yearning for it behind closed doors.

We shame ourselves for our desires, but cannot help ourselves from wanting more.

And in our pursuit for freedom we somehow become enslaved.

A nightmare to so many.

One of the greatest issues to preserving myth is how language's grammatical structures change more quickly over time than vocabulary[2].

In the realm of linguistics, errors plague every area of thought, and they affect everybody from the layman to the intellectual. People waste an enormous amount of time endlessly debating about the "correct definition" for some word (at time of writing, for instance, the world cannot agree on the definition of the word "woman").

Misunderstandings can be resolved rather simply when we grasp that there exist no objective definitions for words.

The word "definition" itself means: "a statement of the *meaning* of a word". Meaning is something the human mind ascribes, it's subjective. And we are always changing the meaning of words—individually and collectively.

In Ancient Greece, for example, the word 'chaos' meant a void or abyss, whereas in a post-modern world the same word is used in the context of disorder and confusion.

Words do not possess meaning by themselves until we make it so, just as the myth of money does not hold truth, until we make it so. And there are no adequate words to encapsulate the word 'money' other than to describe the twisted roots of a tree that run so deep they run the risk of suffocating you in its kitsch.

Across borders, ethnicities, cultures, and religions, money talks the same tongue, yet few tell the original story.

Of the Aztec trading a string of chillies for some cacao beans.

Of the Mongolian securing a new horse for one brick of tea.

Of the tribe offering the firstborn daughter of the chief to a neighboring tribe.

Of the exchange of one thing for another, propelled by desire.

A desire to provide spiritual safety to loved ones who have passed, to expand a palette, for security and power, for basic necessities of food and water.

For thousands of years, before the first coins and paper bills existed, bartering was how humans organized payments for the exchange of goods. From salt to tobacco, to logs, to sex, to dried fish and rice[3]. Eleven-thousand year old clay tokens suggest that even the ancient people of Mesopotamia were keeping tabs of trade[4].

Bartering—to trade one commodity for another—is a beautiful system, but it relies on kinship and trust, impossible at large scale. Consequently, when the agricultural revolution hit roughly ten-thousand years ago and population sizes grew, bartering became cumbersome, giving rise to early monetary systems[5].

Metal rose like fat to the surface, becoming a favored medium. And in the seventh century, the first coin was created by the Lydians made of electrum, an alloy of gold and silver.

This made trade more convenient and effective—especially for the illiterate—giving rise to early democratic systems.

Gold Croeseid, circa 561-546 BC.
Heavy series: 10.76 grams, Sardes mint. Wikipedia

Although the Lydians would eventually be conquered, the coin stuck and soon spread throughout the Mediterranean. Later to morph into paper bills and electronic transactions throughout the world.

Just like folklore, money is a virtual shapeshifter. Literally and figuratively.

It can be both a seashell, paper bill, cacao bean, t-shirt, digital wallet or piece of property. A commodity like silver or a convention like language.

It can be vile, evil, expansive, and rewarding.

Not an actual thing. Not some-thing.

But rather the representation of a thing.

And that thing is value.

You give me your car and I'll give you ten thousand dollars

in exchange. You give me some food and I will give you this gold ring.

Value is defined as the worth or significance of something. How valuable something is is determined through collective agreement and the individual who buys or sells it and how scarce or useful it is to the individual. No good or service has any intrinsic value— it is all subjective, all inventions of the human mind.

For example, water does not spurt forth from the earth with a dollar sign, humans are the ones who assign this.

Likewise, a bottle of water may not be worth much to someone living in a cooler climate who has not exerted themselves and they may be only willing to pay $2 for it. But to someone walking through the desert, who has been exercising vigorously, they may be willing to pay $100.

Even gold, which has obsessed the human mind long before we even had a concept of money, holds no inherent worth.

The colorful pieces of paper we pass around have value only because we all agree to pretend that they do.

And while money is a man-made concept, most humans believe themselves to be nothing without it.

We are taught that money is a gateway to happiness, that having money makes us worthy, and that money is the key to ultimate freedom.

With all of the attributes of a spiritual being. It is intangible and invisible and yet wields great power over our realities.

Worshiped with as much fervor and dedication as any god and, despite it being the most abundant and replenishable resource on earth (we just print more when we need it), there are few things that create more anxieties and frustrations than money.

A myth first born to describe the shift of resources within a population, has become, in its reiteration, a truism of thought that has unsettled the modern imagination and lies in some way out of reach of natural language.

A great illusion.

In Hinduism, māyā is an epithet for goddess Lakshmi, the goddess of "wealth, prosperity and love".

According to Hinduism, the universe we see and experience is not the true reality. It is an illusion created by our minds, which perceives reality in a limited way.

In other words, what we perceive as reality is not the ultimate truth, but a distortion of it.

The idea that the external world is an illusion was greeted by nineteenth century European thinkers as proof of India's inability to cope with the practical world, but as we move into the high-tech era, of ai generated media and virtual realities, our world is becoming more and more like Maya every day. And this experience of illusion permeates all levels, including our daily lives.

We may think we know something about a person, only to later discover deeper layers that had been hidden all along.

We may think we know something about ourselves, only to

find that we are capable of so much more.

It is an obvious fact for all of us—if we but look deeply—that the world is always shifting, changing appearance, hiding something different, deeper, invisible or unknown.

And until we learn to probe beyond these surface waves, we will never find the truth of life and remain deceived, not only by others but also by ourselves.

Reality is known for those who do not think they know, and it is unknown to those who think that they know.

And the deeper layers of reality can never be known by the rational mind. Can never truly be seen through the eyes. Can never be expressed in simple words.

And so, there is a deep meaning to Maya that must be understood for any true self knowledge to develop, for any prosperity to be created.

The world is a magic show, filled with wonder, including depths of wisdom and delight to share with us, if we but part the veil of appearances and look behind not only the forms of the outer world but the movements of our own minds.

This requires us to give up our sense of familiarity, conclusions and opinions, likes and dislikes.

To step back into magical thinking, towards re-enchantment.

And to acknowledge money as the great Maya of our time.

EXERCISE:
THE MYTH OF MONEY

Use this time to take stock of the stories you have been told about money that you have come to believe in.

How would you describe money? What myth do you speak of when you speak of money? What words are synonymous with money to you?

Do you believe that money is scarce and hard to come by?

Do you believe that building wealth requires sacrifice and hard work?

Do you believe that it is unsafe to possess money or that those who have money are evil?

Don't judge or chastise yourself during this exercise, simply recount the stories you have come to absorb and write them down.

Once you have written your beliefs down, keep the piece of paper somewhere safe, we will be referring back to it in later chapters.

4

JEALOUS

"I love money," the man called Jake proclaims to the room, adding: "It's just so easy for me to make." His gold colored BMW is parked in the driveway.

I had met Jake before, on a boat, but the conversation of money had never come up.

Now, seated on cushions at my friend's house, his proclamation of financial ease comes across as gloating. The spit in my mouth sours.

"There's more to life than just money," I murmur.

His shoulders and nose scrunch up, as if saying, Isn't that cute?

I want to leave, sit beneath a tree, but Gee doesn't seem to notice. He's sitting legs sprawled out in front, cap and sunnies on. His bright pink pineapple shirt glows yellow in the light. I watch his face tipped up in oblivion. There is a delicacy to his features that sometimes makes him look younger than he is.

A bonafide Robin Hood, Gee despises those who flaunt their wealth, it was one of the reasons I fell in love with him.

Now it feels like his fate, his deeds, his renouncements, and dislikes have become my own.

Scarcity mindset, I had seethed at him the night before.

Nothing is ever your fault, he'd stormed out. He will go to visit his friend, spend the night, and come back the next day. It's a ritual we have now and we both know how to play the part.

I will cast blame to him, absolving myself of sin, and he will mirror this back.

It's easier to point the finger at others than to point it at myself.

It's easier to distract myself in the making of clay snake figurines than to face the music.

It's easier to renounce something when it feels completely out of reach.

I never used to be this cynical about money. It was something I had happily chased most of my life.

But everything had changed two years back after a mental breakdown had led me to walk away from a multi-million dollar company I had spent seven years building.

Ever since then, I couldn't help but think that money and my pursuit of wealth had been to blame.

If I hadn't been so hell bent on making bank, I never would have found myself trapped, and the depression and subsequent breakdown would never have happened.

If I hadn't desired the things I had desired, I wouldn't have to live through the impending doom scenario facing me now.

Every dawn heralds a new hunt in search of potential culprits. Gee is always at the top of my list, all thanks to the psychic's words.

"Would you take $300,000 over this relationship?" I ask in jest.

"The money," Gee says, poking his tongue out.

"You don't mean that."

"You mean you didn't know that?"

The prosperity spells, the vision boards, the talismans, nothing is working.

Who is responsible?

What is stopping my flow?

Where has my magic gone?

I've played the videos over and over again in my head. Pros and cons lists. But it always just leads to more confusion.

Unopened invoices in my inbox, overdue bills with angry red lettering blazoned across them collecting dust.

I'm sorry I have to let you go, an email to all my contractors, I don't admit I've run out of cash.

From the moment I wake up to the moment I go to sleep, all

I can think about is my pitiful bank account. Flatlining like a hospital monitor. The lower it dips, the lower I go.

An overgrown fantasy gone wrong.

And all of it is, most decidedly, money's fault.

Jake, reminding me that the whole world is willing to chase it blindly.

Curse you all.

Later that evening, after saying our goodbyes, Gee and I head back home along the empty country roads.

"So what did you think?" I ask him.

"Fun." He has forgiven me for the night before.

Snort of derision. "People call some really messed up things 'fun'." I take a deep breath. When did I become so lacking in my play?

"I mean who even says stuff like that out loud?" I recount Jake's audacious proclamation for the sixth time but Gee only responds with a flat "Yea," indicating he's heard enough.

The black tar road dips and snakes forward into the night. I catch myself biting at the dead skin of my thumb. There are a few houses, an abandoned trailer and then nothing for a stretch. A gas station lit up like a UFO crash site appears. He keeps driving. We pass a sign that says Big Trees Plantery and an empty car yard. High in the sky, timid stars kiss and collide.

Gee now solemn in his seat, the happy smile all but gone.
We absorb each other's energy in this way.

Good. Let us suffer together.

The great witch has fallen to her knees.

Money, that is the name of the beast.

DON'T BE JEALOUS

No but seriously…

When you see or hear someone else celebrate their success how do you react?

Truly…deep down?

Are you glad to hear it?

Or do you put up a fake smile while deep down feel your insides crush over themselves?

Does someone else posting about their record revenue months make you cringe and feel frustration?

Do you immediately look for ways to compare yourself?

Do you internally try to belittle them?

…How, surely their marriage must suck, or how they must be depressed behind the scenes.

All so that you can feel better about your own circumstances.

Getting judgmental or bitter when someone else wins is a sure fire way to repel what you desire.

When I was depressed and unfulfilled I quickly became cynical of money and all those who spoke about it openly.

And as a result, I unknowingly (although I should have

known better) hampered the flow of money coming into my own life.

Normalizing success and happiness must include celebrating others when they achieve the great things you aspire to.

Jealousy is always an invitation to transmute to inspiration.

To see these wins as proof that what you seek also exists.

To feel grateful for the thread of evidence that your own manifestation is coming to you.

Pay attention to how you internally respond to others' successes.

Because how you respond will be in direct proportion to how many celebrations you will allow yourself to receive.

5

BULLY

Grit and stone and dirt and bone.

Dragon scratches and curls and unfurls and resurfaces, clipping a talon back into dried mud.

Come, come, Dragon watches a critter string together a sorry web, and bares its sharp teeth. *Go away*.

Gray belly where blue sapphires once shone. Origami made of bruised flesh.

The great beast has burned this world to flames, the dryads cry.

Did you see it? Torching at the great oak.

We must be vigilant.

Master says it is a bully.

Indignation arises, polluting the already sodden forest.

The great beast does not mind.

Treasure or flames, both are in its nature.

Dragon flies high into the sky, casting a shadow that makes the dryads scatter, wings spreading out framed by the two suns that glow like angry furnaces. Tracing roots along the ground, tiny aphids and lice scatter into the air.

Undrained marsh, deep clay and sour pinewood. A wasteland that glows fiery hot.

Featureless and bleak.

The jewels are all but smoldering embers. Diamonds that once glowed like the moon, now dull at the edges.

Insides made of yoke.

Legs that busy themselves cleaning, grooming whiskers and split ends.

Master says, "You seize and withhold my treasure, you deceive me. Have I not destroyed you? I suppose I must destroy you more utterly than you have ever been destroyed before. I will tell all those I encounter to beware, beware of the dragon."

The great beast spews red from its gut.

But Master does not hear.

6

VALUE IS A GREEN

Magic in its essence... is an expression of human hope and confidence, of a morally integrated attitude towards the future. - Malinowski

Studies show that we buy not because we inherently care about the new home or car or travel experience, but because we believe these things will ultimately bring about a sense of wellbeing[6].

Emotion is what drives purchasing behaviors, and also, decision making in general.

We want the beach holiday because we believe it will bring about feelings of relaxation and adventure. We want the new car because we believe it will make us feel more confident, respected or powerful. We want the nanny because we believe it will make us feel more productive and supported. We want the million dollars because we believe it will make us feel playful, free and secure.

Always, what we seek is an expansion in a state of wellbeing.

These are what I call the greens.

Greens are "good feeling" states. States that enhance the parasympathetic nervous system such as joy, pleasure, confidence, adventure, power, and security. There are thousands of good feeling states and even more reasons why we feel them, but they are simple to identify by how they feel in your body. When it feels good, when you *feel* energized, you're in a green state. When it feels bad, when you *feel* depleted of energy, you're in a red state (you can learn more about this inside my first book Magic Source Codes).

Greens communicate to us that our perspective, our train of thought, is aligned to our own path of least resistance. When we are in a green state we are in the process of receiving.

While reds communicate to us what our desires are.

When you feel unfulfilled, you are communicating to yourself in that moment a desire to feel fulfilled. When you are experiencing fear, you are communicating to yourself in that moment a desire to feel courage.

In this way reds are just as important as greens and the point is not to never feel these states of tension for they play a crucial role in guiding us.

The entire myth of money exists only because we aspire to feel better. And what we humans value above all is our greens.

Everything we buy, barter or trade, is done because we are looking to alleviate a red and expand a green. Be it hunger, fear, loneliness, joy, pleasure or pain.

The more something is perceived to expand our greens, the more value we ascribe to it.

For example, a fidget spinner can give you a small dose of pleasure for a few minutes so you may only be willing to pay $15 for it. But a wedding day celebration, that brings about much joy, connection and happiness, is something many are willing to spend tens of thousands of dollars on.

Because money represents value and value is an expansion of greens, the story of money is one that is inseparable to our greens.

If you really want to communicate the value of your product or service to customers, speak about what greens they will experience or expand from working with you. It is one of the most powerful ways to create brand magnetism.

Of course, when our desires feel out of reach or forbidden, certainly it can be tempting to believe that we would be better off without them and this has been a popular stance of many spiritual texts.

In the Hindu tradition, desire is a life force, but also the 'great symbol of sin' and 'destroyer of knowledge and self-realization'. In a similar vein, the second of the Four Noble Truths of Buddhism states that lust, in the broad sense of coveting or craving, is the cause of all suffering.

The Bible opens with a cautionary tale: had Adam and Eve resisted the temptation to eat from the forbidden tree, they and we would not have been banished from Eden.

Four of the seven deadly sins (envy, gluttony, greed, and lust) are centered around desire. Christian rituals such as prayer, fasting, and confession all aim, at least in part, at curbing or regulating desire, as do monastic ideals such as poverty, chastity, and communal living.

The word desire stems from the Latin *desiderare*, 'to long or wish for', which itself derives from *de sidere*, 'from the stars'.

According to the Hindu Rig Veda, the universe began, not with light as in the Judeo-Christian tradition, but with desire, 'the primal seed and germ of Spirit'.

In his masterwork, *The World as Will*, Arthur Schopenhauer says that the whole world is a manifestation of will, including even the human body: the genitals are objectified sexual impulse, the mouth and digestive tract are objectified hunger, and so on.

Everything about us, including our cognitive faculties, evolved for no other purpose than to help us meet the exigencies of desire.

And while this may seem animalistic in nature, studies show that without the continuous stream of desire, there would no longer be any reason to do anything; life would grind to a halt, as is observed in those who suffer from boredom or depression.

Meaning, if you stopped desiring you would fall into apathy.

The human mind cannot exist in sanity unless there is a hope of a future—desires are what form a bridge to future experiences.

A glorious forward motion of the soul that allows us to experience life and all of its lessons.

For it is desire that propels motivation. 'Motivation', like 'emotion', derives from the Latin *movere*, 'to move'.

We were all born out of desire and cannot remember a time when we were without it.

Even those who wish to be free from desire, express a desire.

Our yearnings are a bottomless well, ever changing and ever renewing. Always moving us forward.

Just like the snake, one of the only species on this planet that can never go backwards (its scales simply won't allow it).

For instance, when I was an erotic dancer, I dreamed of someday being taken care of financially by a man. Well, I did end up in this situation and came to quickly realize this was not at all what it was cracked up to be. I hated being dependent on another and having no control over my money and how I spent it. New desires sprang forth and I dreamed of securing myself a steady nine-to-five office job.

I completed my highschool GED, placed myself in University, graduated and landed the office job, only to discover this was also not what I thought it would be. I disliked having to commute two hours each day and only having weekends to do the things I love. And so new desires were born.

I launched a freelancing business and dreamed of one day leading a big team and having my own office space. At the time I worked from home and handled all the day-to-day operations on my own—from accounting to sales through to customer delivery.

Three years into starting the business, I had grown enough to be able to take out a lease on a small office space above a burger joint.

The carpets were old, the walls thin, and it wasn't uncommon to spot the odd cockroach scuttling along the kitchen countertops. But on the glass door that opened up to a stained carpeted set of stairs there was a great big black sticker emblazoned with the logo: Eight Loop Social, and I was proud.

Of course, it didn't take long after moving in for new desires to formulate, and I dreamed of shifting the team into an even bigger, swankier place.

When I eventually achieved this, I soon realized that the big fancy office space, and the massive overheads that came with it wasn't what I really wanted. I was stressed and felt constantly under the pump. And so, again, new desires were born: to own a business with minimal expenses and one that wasn't tied to a lease.

And on and on it goes.

While at first glance it might appear that desires form a void from which we are never satisfied, this is not so. All our desires are refinements based on the previous ones we have experienced and relatively speaking, the desires you hold today are likely a hundred miles ahead of those you held fifteen years ago. The tension exists only when we believe they are out of reach or fall out of gratitude for what already is.

And so, one of the first steps to cultivating wealth is to not only acknowledge our desires but to give ourselves permission to fulfill them, no matter how big or small. No matter how outlandish or irrational. Each one is simply a stepping stone unto the next.

All of them 'stem from the stars', much like gold, which is

mined in natural deposits of the earth and water beds but actually comes from the nuclear fusion of exploding stars called supernovas. When a star reaches the end of its life cycle, it explodes, releasing the heavy elements it has created, including gold, into space.

Your desires are the glitter of the stars.

The waters only murky when we create conditions over what we seek.

EXERCISE: IDENTIFY THE GREENS

Begin to list out all of your financial and material desires. Do not hold back, write down everything without allowing the rational mind to cut you off with "that's impossible" or "how could that ever happen?"

Do you wish to place your children in private school? Do you wish to upgrade or renovate your home? Do you desire to travel more, pay off debts, or to support loved ones?

Write down all your desires knowing that each of these comes straight from source itself. Don't shame or belittle yourself.

Once you have your list, see if you can identify what greens these things will expand in you. Remember, that the money is just a tool to help you cultivate the expansion of your greens, it is never the end game.

For example, if you desire to place your children in private school, perhaps this expands the greens of confidence and peace of mind.

If you desire to travel the world, perhaps this is because you will expand the greens of adventure and play.

If you desire to have savings in your account, perhaps this will expand your sense of security.

Identifying these greens is the first step to making them unconditional.

If you're not sure what it is you even desire right now, use the principle of polarity by simply looking at the reds you are experiencing in your life and what the polar opposite is.

For example, if you are feeling trapped right now, you desire freedom.

If you are feeling confused, you desire clarity.

If you feel insecure or like a failure, you desire confidence.

If you are afraid, you desire play and courage.

If you are overwhelmed and burned out, you desire flow.

If you are depressed and hopeless, you desire gratitude and hope.

Repeat this exercise but in the context of the greens you expand in others (clients or your boss) if you have a business or are looking for a promotion in your job.

Again, keep this list somewhere safe, we will be returning to it later on in this book.

7

RITUALS

Thump.

A bird hits the window waking me from my daydream. Not so much a dream as a nightmare. Incessant thoughts of my own incompetence I can't seem to shake loose.

If I had more money, it would be easy to feel confident once more. To feel playful.

If I had more money, it would be easy to feel secure.

If I had more money, it would be easy to believe in magic.

Drowning, that's what it feels like. Being pushed under water, unable to breathe. Panicked, trampling hooves.

The black bird, now dead on the ground, was the third one this month to commit suicide on my windows and I am almost certain it's a bad omen. *Misfortune*, that's what Google tells me when I search it up. Just what I needed.

When I had launched my new business four months back, it had been a roaring success. I had generated seventy-thousand dollars within a few months and was so confident the success would continue that I had over-invested, stretched myself financially, an exercise that had worked well for me in the past.

But things hadn't gone to plan. Chaos came rearing its head. Dead birds were the least of my worries.

So I list out more suspects. I map out all the things I once did in my last business and connect them like constellations in the sky. A survey of my world. Trying to determine where I am going wrong.

I write out the words '*Sales Team*'. My last company had a sales team of four, perhaps this was the missing link?

My body instantly feels revolted, the thought of having to add more on my plate, when I desire freedom—not overwhelm—feels too backwards.

I scratch out the words, dismayed that I am back at square one. A voice in my head tells me I'm being lazy.

"If I had a million dollars right now, would I still be doing what I'm doing?" I pose the question out loud. "The answer is no."

"Then what?" Gee asks.

I ponder for a moment; the truth is I don't really know. There's a scratching at my soul, a desire to write but it's a slapstick dream, I know writing won't pay all the bills that are piling up like bones in a lion's den. "I'm not sure."

Of course, I may as well have been speaking in abstracts. As far as Gee is concerned, money isn't about passion or flow, it's about waking up in the morning and doing what needs to be done.

He doesn't know the full gravity of my financial situation as we have separate bank accounts.

He doesn't know that I invested thirty thousand dollars on a deposit for a PR company a few months back, hoping they would help grow my business, and that I was now defaulting. Thirty thousand dollars flushed down the drain with nothing to show for.

He doesn't know that the moment I defaulted on that invoice, clients began to mirror this back to me.

He doesn't know that we are living month to month. I shelter him because there's a part of me that thinks he's only with me for the money. I shelter him because I carry shame and too much pride.

"I wouldn't be doing what I'm doing either," He responds flatly. "But we all have to survive somehow."

I can almost hear the ellipsis hanging in the air like a question mark. Insinuating that I should just suck it up, put my big girl pants on, and get to work.

I wish I could force it. And I'm impressed that I had for so many years. But the more I try to promote my new business, the more I force myself to sit down and "do what needs doing", the more I feel myself slipping into the reds.

"I tried doing that in my last business, and well, that almost cost me my life. I learned my lesson, I just can't go down that road again," I say, solemn in my seat.

There's a grim silence. Gee is done trying to convince me. Good.

It bothers me that he feels entitled to give me advice about money when he hardly ever worries about it. When we had first met I had loved the idea of being the main provider, of being a badass boss babe.

I make more in a month than you make in a year. I had told him.

Convincing him to let me pay for everything. Rent, food, gas, dates, travel.

Emasculating him in the process, and making me resent him for it. Now, I no longer know how to untangle myself, without untangling us as a couple.

Defeated, deflated, I do the only thing a witch knows how to do: cast spells.

I gather leaves and twigs from the yard and string them together as talismans.

I burn candles and incense and enchant intentions.

I fill a bucket with warm water and mop the floors. I scrub the bathrooms, the showers and toilets.

I clean spider webs. Spray them down with cleaner first and watch them twitch in the legs till they curl into tiny black balls.

I mop the floors, and empty the bucket of water when flies begin to collect at the top.

Scrubbing, mopping, cleaning, dunking.

I paint and watch the dyes flush down the drain brightly colored as any suicide.

All the while, I pray 'Please send me a sign'. To whom I'm not sure.

I instruct Gee to draw sigils across my breasts and cum all over them.

He obliges and I watch his face as he brings the marker to my skin, hard on against his belly. When he's done I ask him what he wished for. Bodies glistening in sweat.

"Freedom." He says. In that we share the same vision.

It's easy to miss the potion of a witch, it's not always made in a cauldron.

RITUAL: PROSPERITY SPRAY

This ritual will help you to create a potion to invite money through your door.

Aromatherapy has been employed throughout the ages for relief of pain, relaxation, anxiety reduction, and enhanced energy. Lemon, in particular, has been shown in studies to enhance positive mood and also boost norepinephrine release—reducing the body's fight-or-flight response[7].

What You'll Need

- Empty spray bottle
- Lemon or lemon essential oil

How to Do

First charge some water under the full moon. Set the intention of the financial greens you identified in previous chapters.

Clean your front entrance of your home, wipe down any windows and mop the floors, give it a good scrub. Once done, prepare your potion by simply adding the charged water and a few drops of lemon to the mixture. If you like you can add a small citrine crystal to the spray. Citrine is associated with abundance and wealth.

Once your front entrance has been cleaned, spray the air

with your potion. You can recite the following incantation to help you make the intention clear.

"I invite wealth to no end. The money I need the dragon will send. Bills will be paid, my coffers will overflow, my worries released, my wealth will grow. So it shall be, this I make true."

Repeat the incantation three times.

8

UNCONDITIONAL GREENS

Because money is imagined, a myth, that represents our greens, there are infinite ways to cultivate it. The equation is a simple one: expanding money = expanding greens.

Earning it is not that difficult once we comprehend this.

Any and all strategies can work (just as any and all of them can equally fail). And none if it has anything to do with how many followers you have, if you are well connected, what niche your business is in, or what career path you choose. Nor does it have anything to do with how much capital you now have.

Rather it is a reflection of the self-image you hold. The amalgamation of all the stories you tell yourself.

Most people focus on changing the external circumstances of their lives without first transforming the blueprint through which these external circumstances are birthed.

We tell ourselves such things as:

"When I have a bigger bank account, then I will feel at ease."

"When I pay off my debt, then I will feel free."

"When I can purchase that new home, then I will feel secure."

The above are all examples of conditions placed over our greens.

We believe that money will deliver us from our reds, save us.

But for those of you reading this that have come into financial success before, you will know that the dopamine hit that comes from obtaining it is short lived.

Money, contrary to popular belief, can never solve for reds.

In fact studies show time and time again that beyond the basic necessities of Maslow's needs (food and shelter), money does little to boost happiness, not long term anyways.

If you feel unworthy now, you will still feel unworthy with a million dollars in your bank account.

If you feel angry now, you will still feel angry with a new car.

If you feel afraid of money now, you will still be afraid of money after you win the lotto.

If you feel overwhelmed now, you will still feel overwhelmed with a big team.

I came to learn this lesson the hard way. At one stage I went through a phase where I was obsessed with plastic surgery and always it was the same train of thought:

"When I get this surgery, then I will feel beautiful and worthy of love."

It became a never-ending cycle, surgery after surgery.

"Luckily" for me I had a botched operation that caused a lot of issues and had to be operated on three additional times. This put an end to my plastic surgery obsession and forced me to learn to accept and love myself as I was. It wasn't until this happened that I was able to attract love and finally feel worthy.

Chasing money believing it is the thing that will expand your greens is a fallacy and only leads to manic chasing, where it's never enough, nothing fills the void. Over consumption. Dead ends.

Through the years, coaching others, I have been on hundreds of phone calls with entrepreneurs and high creatives facing various dysfunctions and challenges in their lives.

Some had had their children taken away in custodial battles with exes. Some had to deal with health issues or financial difficulty. Some were facing burnout, loneliness or deep unknowns.

Regardless of the resistance or how it had manifested itself into their realities, the response was almost unanimously the same.

The overwhelmed employees or entrepreneurs attempted to combat overwhelm by trying to save time—creating automations, hiring more people, outsourcing, getting through to-do lists etc.

The lonely people attempted to overcome loneliness by trying to find someone to love.

The financially anxious people attempted to solve for the money cinch by doing more things, launching more offers, trying to attract more clients or look for new jobs.

But despite all of these very real and well-intentioned attempts to circumnavigate the chaos, they were all finding themselves looped into much of the same issues. Forever being let down by staff or lovers, always finding themselves in cycles of feast to famine, overcoming one challenge only to be hammered by the next without room to breathe.

No matter the courses taken, actions made, how many mentors or staff are hired, the country or location, different people, different place, same door, same horse.

The reason for this phenomenon is *mirroring.*

What we experience and our circumstances—by and large—are the result of our beliefs. Which, in turn, determine all of our actions and behaviors.

When we believe we are undeserving, we don't ask for pay raises, we don't walk away from dysfunctional relationships, we don't take risks.

When we believe everyone is a cheater or out to get us, we are more suspicious of others, we accuse easily, we have less empathy. Ironically all leading to the very thing we resisted or feared to begin with.

When we are frustrated, we might not say "thank you" to somebody who has just made our coffee. And, not surprisingly, we get frustration back. You see this effect play out in small children who are always perfect mirrors, the more frustrated you are as a parent, the more frustrating your child becomes.

If you believe you are bound to fail, you won't put yourself out there (and create the very scenario of failure). If you believe you are really bad at saving money, you'll create situations where you confirm this idea. Maybe you'll get yourself into debt, maybe you'll attract circumstances where unexpected bills come in to take all your savings away.

Consider the list you wrote from Chapter 3 around your own beliefs of money, how have these been reflected back to you in your own life experiences?

Mirroring is what I experienced when I defaulted on the invoice for the PR company, clients quickly reflected this back, defaulting on their own payments. When we are late on paying our invoices, others will also delay paying us.

If we judge others—whether that is for having money, or their content or style of business—we ourselves will come to experience being judged. By the way, when we are afraid of being judged this is actually a form of judgment, for to suspect or expect judgment from others, is to judge others. We are social creatures, and our desire to fit in within the tribe is stronger than our desire for money. So as long as we judge or fear judgment, we will prevent ourselves from receiving.

Mirroring is also why one should never try to earn money by scamming or harming others. This will always backfire in one way or another.

The outer world is like a projector screen. Fighting with the projector—trying to manipulate or altar it, doesn't help you to actually change it. It is akin to fighting our own reflection.

Money represents an expansion of greens, holding conditions over these greens therefore gets us nowhere.

The fastest way to cultivate wealth is to become a match, to embody the greens that we desire, unconditionally.

Meaning, if you desire freedom, you must embody freedom now. Not tomorrow, not next week, not when the client pays the invoice. Now.

If you desire security, you must embody security now.

If you desire confidence, you must embody confidence in the present moment.

This doesn't mean you need to be happy all the time, or never experience reds. On the contrary, you can be unhappy and still make bank, but you must match the greens you seek to obtain through money.

We are vibrational beings, both signal and antennae, and it doesn't matter how good your sales copy or offer is, if you are trying to expand play in others, yet you yourself live disconnected from this state, customers and leads will pick this up from a mile off and be repelled by what you're selling. They won't know why rationally but their "spidey senses" will alert them. On the flip-side, if you are expanding play in others and are deeply connected to play, unconditionally, you will become a magnet to leads and opportunities. It won't matter if you have typos, messy sales pages or half-formulated offers, it will somehow work.

Cultivating wealth, getting to the income brackets that you want, calling in the money that you desire, begins by recognizing that your financial and material desires are always motivated by an expansion in wellbeing and that there exist no conditions over your greens.

You get to have the abundance, the freedom, the joy, and pleasure, right now.

Yes, right now.

Because you, my friend, are in command of a superpower innate to you.

THE CHASE

And so I chase,

The stars, the switchbacks, the sex.

The thunder of my running shoes on an empty path.

The money, the accolades, the ego.

The palm that will fit perfectly into mine.

Living life on the border of something less than real.

For it is here I find respite

From an old-time friend

The androgynous dark

That curls it's lips with desire

And promises of the universe

"Come" it will say.

Perhaps someday I will

But for now,

I chase.

9

WISH DRAGON

"What you seek is seeking you" - Rumi

Drowsy, night-chilled, and twisting myself from sleep in the early dawn. This is how each night has been lately, restless and mired in fretfulness. I wake up feeling like I've been hit by a truck.

The home is still cloaked in shadows as I shuffle into the kitchen, while my children stir in their rooms. I catch a glimpse of my son in his bed, his breath steady and fluid, a cheek catching the soft rays of morning light. How I wish I could have the peace of mind of a child, without care or worries of the entanglements of money.

I cannot get the email out of my mind. It was from my accountant, informing me that there is forty thousand dollars owed for taxes from my last company two years back.

Panicked I had called him right away, *how can this be?* I'd asked, the blood drained from my face. He had explained how the oversight had happened but this didn't make it go away. I would have screamed then and there, if my throat had not closed up in fear. Where am I supposed to get the money from? The dead bird now a manifested bad omen.

And now, despite a dawn wind lifting an impressive cloudscape above the green pastures outside, a duck-egg sky striated gold and pink, my accountant's words are all I can think of.

How had it all come to this?

I turn the kettle on and begin rummaging through the fridge, nudging the bread and butter out of the way so that I can retrieve the tray of caramel slices Gee made earlier in the week. I don't hear the footsteps behind me—the hum of the kettle is too loud—so I start like a cat when my daughter calls "Good morning mummy."

Clogged and barely awake, even she can see the worry etched across my face.

"Are you ok?" She asks.

A half-hearted fake smile, I respond, "I'm ok love."

I promised myself I would never let my children hear me complain about money, only because I myself was raised in households where the adults always worried and stressed about it. My mother fretting over a bill, left unopened on the table, my father complaining how he never had any. And I know how—as a child—I came to absorb my parents' financial anxiety as if it were my own.

I carried these narratives for the majority of my adult life and it took me a lifetime to unravel them.

Now, I carry the weight of the world on my shoulders alone.

My daughter, oblivious to the internal sniping of my mind,

shrugs and rolls herself onto the sofa, grabbing at the remote.

On the counter is a letter from the City Council, informing me that my property rates payment is due, another two thousand dollars owed. If I stop opening these letters maybe they will just go away.

Sales are still dead in the water. The only revenues coming in are from recurrent payments from existing clients and even these have started to dwindle. I'm resentful of coaching as an industry, which makes it impossible for me to promote my offers. Even though I know I'm a powerful teacher when I'm "turned on", even though my clients gain tremendously from working with me. I shun this part of myself.

I've stopped trying to promote anything. Now, my strategy is simply to bury my head deep down for long enough and hope that it will all just go away.

I know I need to figure it out soon.

I know I need to get to the root of my money problems.

I need to stop desiring things.

I need to just give up.

This is the demented dance of my mind. Round and round, up and down.

The more I try to "heal" my money blocks, the more I begin to slip into the reds of anxiety. Reds with sharp teeth that glint back at me, hungry and waiting to devour me whole.

I remember this feeling well; the same edginess is what had

started the whole downward spiral a couple years before. Now it feels like I am repeating the whole thing again. What is the point of any of it?

Across the mantle, the dried snake figurines stare back passively. A pile of ashes from the incense burned from my last ritual.

Show me a sign, anything, I had pleaded.

I hand my daughter a glass of milk, pulling my bathrobe tightly around me, shivering at the thought of that forty-thousand-dollar tax bill. An idea crosses my mind.

Walking into the office, I pull open a drawer stuffed with bent and worn journals. For as long as I have been able to write, I have been keeping journals. Now they occupy various crevices and corners of the house like silent ghosts of my past.

Above the desk is a vision board, printed colored images of the desires I once had. A hot tub, a new kitchen, a notification from the bank that my mortgage has been paid off in full. I feel the heat of the images glaring at me, accusing and taunting.

There's a book with an ocher leather casing, dated from 2005. I flip through its pages and find an entry with sad capitalized lettering that says "I HATE MY LIFE!!!!". And then below it: *A client paid me $900 today to dress up in a wedding dress while he recited the Bible back to me. What is happening to me?*

There's another page with a dragon sketched across it. It looks powerful and regal. I think nothing more of it and stuff the diary back into the drawer, unwilling to revisit this part of my history and all of its incriminating evidence.

I find the journal I am looking for. It has a silver cover and a cartoon cow on the front. Penned to the first page is the date 2019. Most of the entries are of to-do lists, with scribbled out words and random thoughts like: *Why doesn't the little pig girl wear a mask when they are out, makes no sense???*

There are pages upon pages of gratitude lists. At surface level, if one were to read this journal, they would likely get the impression that its author was a well-balanced and happy individual. But I know better. That this was the year when the depression had really begun to rear its head, when the finances had started to dwindle and the same panic facing me now had begun to set in.

I'm searching, rather hoping, to find clues, something, anything, to reveal to me breadcrumbs to solve for my current circumstances. One entry catches my eye:

I know the money issue is a lack of integrity with my business—truth is it no longer inspires me, I'm BORED of talking about ads. I'm tired of working all day and always thinking about to-do lists. I keep telling all my clients to follow their passion, that that is where the money lies, but here I am—behind the scenes, feeling trapped and too scared to follow my own advice. I don't even know what it is I desire to do, how am I supposed to trust myself forward? There is no way out, I just need to suck it up and keep doing what I'm doing.

I place the journal back down, my fingers curling as if burned by the pages.

Like a clairvoyant seeing into the future, I already know what would follow. That six months after writing the entry I would go on to attempt suicide, on multiple occasions, and walk away from the business.

The words tug at my heart and I want to reach out across the web of time and console this younger version of myself. Tell her that she is free to walk away, that she MUST walk away, for her own sake.

A thought occurs to me that a future version of myself is telling me these exact same words in this moment.

"Mum, can I have breakfast?" My son asks, standing in his underwear at the door, breaking the spell.

I place the journal back into the drawer, my mind whirling, and lead him into the kitchen where my daughter is watching a movie.

On the screen, a chunky man holds a green teapot while driving a car at high speed.

"Ah, dragon guy, I summon you," the man says, "I want enough puppies to open a puppy store!" The car jolts and a dragon appears from thin air.

"Yes puppies," the dragon agrees, "And it shall be so!" With this, puppies begin to appear magically into thin air, filling every compartment of the car.

The sounds fade away, memories tug at the edges of my being.

Dragon, I feel my mouth form the word. It feels soft and sweet as a cherry rolled upon my lips. The juice of it wetting my tongue. I say it again.

Somewhere on the astral plane, there is a glimmer of a tail.

It moves fluidly through the air. Through fractals of geometry.

PERCEIVING ABUNDANCE ALL AROUND

Most of us are so fixated on the money we don't have, on the wealth that isn't acquired yet, that we completely neglect to notice how wildly abundant a twenty-first century life already is.

A simple, yet powerful, exercise to help you intentionally shift your focus away from a present reality of lack and scarcity is to shift your focus towards the abundance already existing all around you, to notice it in its physical manifestation.

Consider this: most ancient humans and even your great-grandparents had a staple diet of beer and bread. If they were lucky they would get an apple for Christmas.

These days, we walk into any modern grocery store and have thousands of options. Fifteen different soy milks, off-season vegetables and fruits flown halfway across the world, and meats that would previously only be afforded by kings or the wealthy.

The entire exercise of grocery shopping, one that is normally seen as a banal waste of time, is an opportunity to revel in abundance.

The next time you walk into your grocery store, really take a moment to marvel at all the choices available to you. Walk through the aisles in wonder and awe for all the options.

The next time you take a hot shower, take note of how lucky you are to have this experience.

The next time you step outside, notice how abundant the air is. Something that your entire being depends on, yet you never really give it much of a second thought.

It is only when we come to lose our hot water, or when the shelves of the grocery store are emptied, that we come to appreciate just how fortunate we were when we had these.

But it shouldn't, and need not, get to the stage of losing it all to find gratitude for that which already exists.

When we are out of gratitude, non-perceptive, to the abundance existing already, it is very difficult, if not impossible, to cultivate more of this in our lives. For the simple reason that our focal point determines our emotions.

By the same token, start to take stock of *threads*.

Threads are those things that show up around you as proof that what you want is coming your way. Evidence that what you desire exists.

For example, if you desire a Lamborghini, a thread would be to see one driving past.

If you desire a million-dollar business, a thread could be someone on your newsfeed sharing their seven-figure celebration.

If you desire to make loads of money, without lifting a finger, a thread could be coming across or being introduced to someone who came into a sudden and unexpected windfall of cash.

If you desire love, take notice and appreciate the lovers that walk down the street.

Usually our big desires will begin manifesting themselves as threads around us first.

Getting triggered or jealous by threads is a surefire way to prevent the real deal from coming into our lives.

It is very important that we not only become perceptive to these but that we celebrate and acknowledge them when they do show up.

10

IMAGINE DRAGONS

"Logic will get you from A to B. Imagination will take you everywhere."
- Albert Einstein

In the ancient city of Babylon, amidst its towering ziggurats and bustling markets, there lived a fearsome dragon known as Mušḫuššu. The people of Babylon spoke of the creature with awe and trepidation, for its legend was intertwined with the city's founding and its powerful gods.

Mušḫuššu was no ordinary dragon; it was a creature of divine origin, created by the great god Marduk himself. Its body was adorned with shimmering scales, glistening like emeralds in the sun. It had the forelegs of a lion, sharp claws, and a serpent-like tail, which bore a venom capable of subduing even the mightiest of foes. With wings that stretched wide, Mušḫuššu soared through the skies like a celestial guardian.

The Babylonians revered Mušḫuššu as a symbol of divine protection, a guardian spirit that watched over their city. It was believed that the dragon's presence brought good fortune and warded off evil spirits.

And the Babylonians weren't the only ones keeping company with a dragon.

The ancient Babylonian creation myth of Tiamat (left dates to at least the second millennium B.C).

Across all cultures and all geographics, the dragon has pierced through the imagination of humankind in some form or another.

In Chinese mythology, dragons were depicted as long, serpentine creatures with scaled bodies, benevolent creatures associated with good fortune, power, and wisdom.

In European folklore, dragons were often portrayed as fearsome beasts: large, scaly creatures with wings, associated with hoarding treasures and guarding them fiercely.

We still cannot fully explain why every human society has imagined dragons, despite having little cultural exchange.

Some believe that the dragon is a representation of what is dangerous about this world, a creature that mimics the snakes in the bushes, ready to ambush[8].

Another theory stipulates that ancient people misinterpreted the fossils of extinct creatures (such as the Tyrannosaurus rex) and came to imagine great flying beasts that breath of flames[9].

Regardless of the origin of inspiration, almost universally, dragons have come to tap into deep-seated human fears, desires, and aspirations.

They hold the keys to piles of gold, but watch your footing for they could equally burn you to a crisp.

Our ability to picture these creatures is all thanks to the enlarged portion of our brains called the neocortex.

Responsible for creative and cognitive abilities, such as language, symbolism, and memory, it is here that we find the seat of imagination—the superpower innate to all humans. Responsible for all innovation, invention, and art. Responsible for all myth and folklore.

The faculty within us capable of piercing through Maya.

According to William Mahony, the root of the word Maya stems from *man*—or "to think"—implying the role of imagination in the creation of the world. In early Vedic usage, the term implies, states Mahony, "the wondrous and mysterious power to turn an idea into a physical reality".

The imagination is the true expression of the divine feminine in our consciousness. The realm of knowing which comes through dreams, intuition, and voices of the body.

It is through the imagination that we see the unseen.

That we connect with the impossible.

That we venture beyond existing structures.

And form mental images of those things not perceived through the five senses.

Unfortunately, very few human beings realize how cut off they are from the power of their most important faculty of expression.

At some point in our lives, we stopped playing and having fun like we did as children.

Keith Johnson, author of "*Impro*", once wrote that there is no such thing as an adult, only atrophied children. And it's true. There is no magical line you cross into adulthood; you just get really good at pretending to be one.

It takes a lifetime of rigid education, peer pressure, deadlines, monetary constraints and workplace conformity to slowly beat your inner child into submission. But at what cost?

Somewhere along the line, we stopped using our imagination, and with it went our capacity to reinvent and play with the infinite realm of possibilities.

Instead, we imagine the economy crashing or what might happen to our kids, our businesses, or our jobs—doomsday scenarios—and it causes a real and measurable negative physiological impact on our bodies and our wellbeing.

We imagine our partners leaving or betraying us and we *feel* stressed or suspicious. We fabricate failures we're sure we'll encounter and we *feel* stuck, preventing ourselves from moving forward.

It's estimated that the average person daydreams over two thousand times per day, each lasting on average fourteen seconds[10]. But because the human brain is a bona fide natural problem-solving machine that fixates on worst-case scenarios and issues at hand, the imagination, when left unmanaged, can spin us into circuits of the past. It stunts growth and pumps cortisol through our system. It can make us believe in the Maya right in front of us and turn our daydreams into nightmares.

The power of our imagination is such that we are often unable to distinguish the experience of emotion from physiological sensations that accompany affect[11]. It can elicit all of the reds and all of the greens.

In other words, what we imagine *feels* just as real as those sensations caused by external events.

So much so that holistic research into "guided imagery" now reveals that to 50 percent of surgical patients undergoing positive imagery have a reduced use of pain medication and lower length of hospital stay[12] and that cancer patients participating in positive imagery experience longer remission[13].

Both superpower and Achilles heel.

The good news is that—if you are intentional about it—you can teach yourself to command and harness the power of your imagination.

You can use it to remove any and all conditions over your greens, so that you can command forth that which you desire.

And the same muscle used to imagine dragons, is the one used to invent money.

EXERCISE:
IMAGINE YOUR DRAGON

Use this moment to flex that powerful imagination of yours by defining and creating your dragon.

Consider what your dragon might look like. What color is it? What is its skeletal structure like? Is it bipedal with two strong legs and smaller arms, or does it walk on four legs? Does it have big wings or small ones? Is it covered in fur or scales?

More importantly, consider your dragon's personality traits. Is it regal? Playful? Clumsy but loyal? See if you can concoct a personality that feels safe, green, and fun and then ascribe it to your money.

If you want to take this exercise up a notch, create a visual representation of your dragon through your medium of choice.

Studies show that when we are engaged in any type of visual creative expression: drawing, painting, collaging, sculpting clay, writing poetry, knitting etc, we activate reward pathways in the brain and lower stress levels[14].

There is no right or wrong way to imagine your dragon, and what you create is just for you so don't worry if you don't consider yourself artistic by nature.

The point of this exercise is to help you stretch your creative capacities in a way that fosters affinity towards money.

11

WAITING

Dragon flicks serpentine coils in a wet explosion across the water then disappears into the orbs of the sky. Belly trembling, breath like a metallic rattle.

The dryads all the while murmuring, of course they murmur. All the way back to the burnt trees.

Sharing news of the previous night's casualties. Like birds regurgitating a meal. Willows have been uprooted and torn, strangling themselves, sap leaking. Peonies up in smoke and the mountains smoldering.

Oh it hurts.

That nasty beast.

Dragon tumbles through the air, clumsy in flight, shooting up on plumes of heat rising, and dropping on shafts of cool air sinking.

Soaring, soaring, soaring. Flowing and rippling, a trail of smoke in its wake.

There are shapes and scents of others, but only Master smells like home.

Splatch, splatch, the sound of mud squelched underfoot.

A contradictory creature: steeped in the technical world of anatomy and yet well-versed in the magical.

Waiting, waiting, waiting. In an empty cave of broken Fabergé.

Cursing and weeping, lips pulled back in a terrible snarl, Dragon mimics it all.

Like an angry fog, that eats its way through the sky, through the spaces between things, obscuring the light. It smells of river: silt and brackish water, of fish and mangroves. Rolling across the land as if nothing else existed turning all who venture into the forest into a ghost.

A rabbit carcass, piles of bones.

Drunk on another world.

Master commands, and Dragon obeys.

12

THE DIVINE FEMININE

"Imagination is the star in man, the celestial or supercelestial body."
Ruland

When you think about your bank account, how do you feel?

When you think about paying your bills next month, how does this feel?

The way we feel, our emotions, represents our prominent focus or perspective.

And most of us, unwittingly, engage the divine feminine from the reds. Meaning, when we think about our desires or money it doesn't feel good.

We dislike money as a construct, we are unhappy with our own financial circumstances.

We fear there will not be enough, we imagine scenarios of doom and gloom and contemplate on all our past failures.

Unknowingly commanding forth more reds and reasons to be stressed.

Most of us like to believe we are in affinity with money when really we are abusive to our dragons.

We fixate on all the things it does wrong or incorrectly, its inadequacies and faults.

Let me ask you this: if you entered a relationship with this predisposition how do you think this relationship would end?

If you didn't trust your partner enough to go out with friends for a night, if you always chastised them, if you were always grumpy and upset at them, letting them know how they are not good enough for you, or evil—how healthy would this relationship be?

Likely it would end very badly, and you would be called a narcissist at the end of it.

You would end up blaming all men or women and find yourself circuited into much of the same experiences over and over again, believing that everyone else is to blame.

Money is no different to a good friend or a partner.

It requires us to meet it with love, trust, and gratitude.

With kinship and playfulness.

When we focus on what we don't want, we attract the very thing we are in resistance to.

Our actions and behaviors will mirror this back, and our financial circumstances become the manifestation of this focal point.

So if your bank account is declining, if clients are defaulting, if money feels hard—likely, it is because you yourself are not in affinity with what you actually desire.

You say you want more money, but then you spend your days resenting its existence, fearful or spiteful of it. Searching for culprits, as I once did.

When we are searching for reasons, or perceiving the ways in which money is not working in our favor, this is a red because it *feels* bad in the body to think of money in this way. When we think that we are incomplete, or that we don't deserve money, this is also a red for it does not *feel* good to hold such perspectives. When we think we are stuck or that we must sacrifice ourselves in order to receive, this is a red for it *feels* like hardship. When we are afraid of being judged for having money, this is a red for it *feels* like a contraction.

It's all well and good to perform rituals and affirm ourselves of our abundance, but so long as we are thinking of money in red, we can only ever attract more flames.

You don't need to heal anything, you don't need to be perfect, you don't need to be the most intelligent person, you don't even need to be happy or be a good person.

There is evidence of money flowing to those who lack all of the above, none of these are conditions to wealth (although, as mentioned, do not obtain money unethically for this will only be mirrored back to you).

You only need to think and feel green about your money.

This simple tweak is often enough to create a substantial shift in your financial circumstances.

I have seen clients suddenly create an influx in leads and sales—with no outward change in their strategy or messaging. Others who have literally found or been given money in strange and unusual ways. Invoices that were long past due, suddenly paid.

To expand our wealth we must play with the divine feminine within the greens. To not only allow ourselves to desire big things, but to feel good about these things.

If our desires are rooted in reds, we create imbalance and command flames.

For instance:

"I want more money so that I *don't* go broke."

"I want more money so that I *don't* have anxiety".

These examples above are how many of us construct our desires. We are seeking to fix a red, and red is all that will ever come back from such a scenario.

I wanted to renovate my kitchen because I was ashamed and embarrassed of it. The desire to renovate was really a desire to experience more confidence, but it was being driven and engaged from a space of lack. A red. And so because of this, it felt almost impossible to save the money required to complete the renovations.

A lot of people struggle to save money. Not because it's hard to save money. People with lots of money can struggle to save so saving is irrelevant to how much you make. They struggle simply because saving is not exciting or fun to them—they hold no affinity to it. Even if they say they wish to save, they feel anxiety over their shortfall of savings, and feel a sense of duty or unworthiness because they don't have it.

A great analogy I once heard referenced to by Genevieve Rackham in her book Sexy Money is to think about eating a chocolate cake. When you think about eating such a cake, your mouth salivates, your heart rate rises, you get excited. You wouldn't be thinking about chocolate in the sense that you're starving and angry and pissed off at it. Rather it's a forward thinking of how delicious it will taste, how much you will savor it. It grows an appetite but it's not an uncomfortable one, rather it's a pleasant one.

Your desires should feel the same way.

"I want more money because I *do want* to experience new layers of freedom."

"I want the new kitchen because I *do want* to enjoy so many beautiful memories with my family."

By the same token, the myths and beliefs we hold around money should also be rooted in greens.

"I have to hit rock bottom to make it big."

"Money is evil."

"I will be judged for having money."

All of these are beliefs rooted in reds.

Consider the list of beliefs you outlined in Chapter 3. Are these grounded in greens or reds? If the latter, this is the reason why things are feeling financially strained for you.

It is impossible to solve scarcity while being focused on scarcity. Our creative capacities are such that our dragons can never go against our free will.

If you're guilty of engaging the divine feminine in red, don't be, the truth is most of humanity is in the same boat.

A consequence of myth mired through the passage of time and the manipulation of language.

Your dragon deeply desires to serve you. But it cannot understand your words, it does not speak the human tongue, it works purely from the energetics of your own being.

The vibrations of how you feel.

And the way you feel first starts with your perspective and thoughts, how you imagine reality.

And while it's true that all intentions stem from the cauldron of the divine feminine, and that rooting these in green can be enough to shift the flow of money in your life—just as the double helix, it takes two to tango.

APPRECIATING MONEY

Want more money in your life?

Here's something you should know:

Gratitude and scarcity are two vibrations that cannot coexist at the same time.

One of these is rooted in red, the other in green.

One of these will attract money, the other will repel it.

Most of us spend our days worried, stressed and frustrated about the money (or lack thereof in our lives.

Emitting strong vibrational signals of scarcity and, unsurprisingly, finding ourselves looped into more financial frustration.

In other words, when we think of money, it is done in red emotional states (ie: states that stress the nervous system).

To overcome this, stop looking for ways in which money isn't working for you or going right and instead shift into a space of deep gratitude for your dragon, for gratitude is the strongest expression of a green.

It sounds too simple to work.

But I promise you this is the secret and how I have been able to build three seven figure businesses.

Do this for even just two weeks and you'll completely change your financial circumstances.

Remember: What you appreciate appreciates.

13

DEAR UNIVERSE

Dear Universe,

Being the true witch that I am, I Cat Howell, give here a true relation of all that has befallen me recently.

With this account, I hereby relinquish authority and hand the reins of my fate over to you. Something perhaps I should have done a long time ago.

As you know, I have felt so, so lost of late. Abandoned by magic itself.

For what good is magic if it cannot even help you keep the roof over your own head?

And so it was that I asked you for a sign, and a dragon was shown. Stirring memories of a time before, though I could not place my finger on it fully. It woke me in the middle of the night, so important I was sure I wouldn't forget it, but, in the fog of morning, it was gone.

At first I did not not know what it all meant.

Dragons are greedy, lustful, spiteful things. Was this a joke you intended to play on me?

But the dragons you have revealed to me were of a different sort. Playful, jubilant, loyal, dropping bad dad jokes.

So I took myself into the forest to ponder it all, extrovert my perspective amongst the tall birch and pine, canopies scraping at the sky.

No one else was around, and I admit, I was still feeling much confusion and frustration for my circumstances.

Things have not been easy.

I've been angry with Gee, blaming him for my problems, each night we argue. I've been angry with money, how it has enraptured the world in this capitalistic society. I've been angry with myself for laying waste to something that had once been all I ever desired.

Stopping my walk, deep in the woods, no one around. I let out a giant bellow. Taking the wind out from my lungs with only the trees and fluttering birds to witness me (and my dog, who was covered in mud from the legs down). I had not screamed in such a way for a long time. It was an instant relief.

And so I screamed once more, releasing it all. It was not joy, but nor was it anger. A cry with no right angles, no rules, but with many notes at once.

And that's when I remembered it. The dragon of a time long before. When I was just a young woman, lost in this world. Memories that echoed through the trees. The one sketched in the journal.

Just as I did, thunder rolled through the clouds. A rumbling, as if my cries had been heard from above.

One droplet, and then another. Then the rain came pouring down.

I held my face up to the sky and let the water fall across my cheeks.

As if possessed I hopped and whirled, swinging round trunks, heels grinding into mud. The air sliding ribbons through my hair. Inspired into a strange metamorphosis.

The leaves rustled and the fog that had haunted me began to lift.

I saw.

I see.

That financial freedom is a feeling.

A state of being.

I felt.

I feel.

And while, I don't fully understand yet how this will come to help me: my mortgage is due, debt is up to my eyeballs, my mind demands answers.

I hereby diplomatically refuse to bend to its dour mood.

From heronout, my money is a dragon, and my dragon is my money.

Thank you for the guidance.

Yours truly

Cat

14

DEEPENING THE DIVINE FEMININE

Others believe in prayer…have not all yet learnt that to ask it is to be denied? Let it be the root of your Gospel. Oh ye, who are living other people's lives! Unless desire is subconscious, it is not fulfilled, no, not in this life." - Austin Osman Spare

At around three pounds, the gelatin like tissue in your skull accounts for only a couple of percent of your total body mass, but it consumes a lot of energy—some 20 percent of the calories you eat every day.

Conscious thought is "expensive" in energy terms. To compensate for this the brain tends to shift its more costly processing tasks towards automated, "cheaper" routines.

It's estimated that 95 percent of our brain activity is unconscious, meaning that the majority of the decisions we make, the actions we take, our emotions and behaviours, depend on brain activity that lies beyond conscious awareness[15].

When conceptualizing the unconscious mind, it can be helpful to compare the mind to an iceberg. Everything above the water represents conscious awareness while everything below the water represents the unconscious.

Consider how an iceberg would look if you could see it in its entirety. Only a small part of the iceberg is actually visible above the water. What you cannot see from the surface is the enormous amount of ice that makes up the bulk of the iceberg, submerged deep below in the water.

The things that represent our conscious awareness are simply "the tip of the iceberg." The rest of the information that is outside of conscious awareness lies below the surface.

While this information might not be easily accessible consciously, it is possible to directly influence what lies beneath.

In 1913 Carl Gustav Jung developed a procedure for inducing visions that he termed “active imagination”[16]. Combining hypnagogic states with visualizations to induce waking hallucinations, his process was adopted and modified widely in the Western occultism and New Age spirituality.

This pairing of visions and altered consciousness is termed “gnosis”, meaning knowledge of the divine. This was the drawcard that pulled me into the world of alchemy.

You see, while I had been an avid follower in manifestation and mindset practices for many years, I often found the results to be inconsistent and lackluster.

I would affirm positive beliefs to myself over and over again but always there would be a little voice in the back of my head that would sneer “Yea right”.

Mostly because these beliefs were supplanted deep below my

conscious awareness.

When I began to explore the world of magic, and came across gnosis as a method to set intentions into the subconscious, to influence the divine feminine, everything changed.

A state of gnosis is an altered state of consciousness or an "out of mind" experience. Alchemists use this state as a way to leave rational thought behind and access the subconscious to recode beliefs. It is often described as heightened levels of intuition, creativity and spiritual awareness. It feels like a sense of unity, present moment, transcendence from the material world, and a deep sense of inner peace and clarity.

When we set intentions that are rooted in green from this space, incredible things happen.

There are thousands of ways to enter gnosis.

Some of my personal favorites include: breathwork, ecstatic dancing, orgasm, sensory deprivation (such as float tanks), cold plunges (although this one is probably my least favorite) and psychedelics.

The latter may be the oldest psychopharmacological agents known to man, with cave art from modern-day Algeria depicting ritualistic mushroom consumption as far back as 9000 BCE[17].

It is suspected that the Ancient Greeks would consume a drink called kykeon, made of psychoactive fungi, during their revered Greek Mysteries festival celebrating the magic of life, and that the Eucharist also involved the use of psychedelics[18].

Artifacts depicting Osiris holding out a blue lotus lily (*nymphaea caerulea*), a psychoactive plant consumed as a tea and legal in most countries, show that even the great pyramid builders weren't opposed to getting help to enter altered states.

If psychedelics feel uncomfortable for you, don't force yourself to do something that doesn't feel right. There are countless other drug-free alternatives and discovering what works best for you is a process of dating yourself.

Anything involving flow is a state of gnosis, so when you are lost in time doing even mundane things like washing a car, or building something that compels you, you have entered the imprintable area of the subconscious.

Likewise, play and gratitude are powerful autotelic states.

The more you enter these states, with intention, the more you will remove conditions over your greens and come to receive those things that match with this biochemical vibration.

The clearer the signal you send to your dragon.

EXERCISE: HYPNAGOGIC LIGHT

Hypnagogic light is another method of entering gnosis and uses a flickering light technique.

It is a method that has been used since ancient times, through spinning wheels in dark caves with a burning fire.

When early neurophysiologists first started using it, they found that several individuals reported that the flickering lights induced visual hallucinations through closed eyelids.

Although remarkable, the hallucinations gained relatively little interest within the laboratory. But as the 1960s underground heard about the psychedelic-like effects and visuals produced by a mere stroboscope, it was eagerly welcomed as a tool for enlightenment and a legal, drugless high.

The short-term alterations in consciousness and kaleidoscopic patterns induced by the flickering lights even inspired some to manufacture their own devices, such as painter and poet Brion Gysin's *Dreamachine*.

For most people, the sensations created by hypnagogic light effects and hypnagogia are very pleasant. Resulting in complex cryptic pictures and sounds. And these can cause spontaneous creativity, messages from unknown parts of your unconscious mind, and a feeling of deep relaxation blended with heightened awareness afterwards.

Today, these stroboscopic lamps are often called hypnagogic

light lamps, with the word hypnagogic referring to the transitional state from wakefulness to sleep.

Thankfully, you do not need to find a cave or purchase expensive lights because we have advanced technology available to us these days, such as phones and Youtube channels, that can produce much the same effect.

Please do not attempt this exercise if you have epilepsy.

What You Need

- Google cardboard (this can be purchased for a few dollars online—it is also optional)
- Your phone
- Flickering lights video (you can search Youtube and will find thousands—there are also apps such as *DreaMachine* which assist with this as well)

How to Do

Load the video on your phone and insert the phone inside of the Google Cardboard. Lie down somewhere in a comfortable position and listen to isochronic or binaural beats through headphones. Close your eyes as the lights begin to flicker.

Once the altered state has been achieved (you'll know once you start feeling calm and/or seeing images through your closed eyelids), turn your gaze inwards to your desires, the list you wrote in Chapter 6—see if you *feel* the greens you listed out.

15

COMING OUT

Two hundred thousand dollars.

That's what the lawyer tells me I could owe due to a possible contract issue from my last company. The tidal waves just keep coming.

No matter, I have a dragon on my side. Round bellied and glittering scales. It incinerates my world, but I try to bestow it with kindness.

I surrender, I surrender.

I hold my shoulders back, picturing this powerful beast behind me, swirling, building momentum, traveling across dimensions to 'fetch' the amounts needed. I am gentle with it. When thoughts that taste like reds come up, I reframe them.

It seems ludicrous to imagine my money as a fictional character, but no more than the ludicrousness of my financial circumstances.

My rational mind stutters at the thought. It tells me that I need to be worried, that I should be stressed out, losing sleep, that I should grind myself into a pulp until I bleed out, because that is how money is earned—not through imagined characters.

But something begins to shift in me.

I begin to make small repayments to all those owed, as much as I can possibly stretch, in full trust that the money will replenish itself.

And slowly, as a worm dips its head from a trunk, with nothing to lose anymore, the conversations with my clients begin to change.

I am a witch, I tell the world. *Haven't you heard I grew horns?*

Full blown confession.

I no longer care if there is backlash, the shame is all but swept to the side, I guess that is the gift that comes from being cornered.

Spurred on, I book myself into a magical photoshoot (even though I can't really afford to). I tell the photographer to "make me look like a sorcerer". Velvet green cape, alone in the forest. I record a guided meditation of my dragon (you can listen to it on Youtube, called "How to Command a Blue Money Dragon") and I publish the pictures online, there is no turning back.

And while some people are deeply offended by my admission (I guess they miss the old version of me, the one that talked about ads and agencies and building teams), my confession surprises no one more than myself.

Messages begin to inundate my inbox, people professing their own interest in magic.

I shift my business away from cut-and-dry mindset approaches and into conversations of alchemy and launch a coven. The resistance I once felt towards the coaching industry lifts. My sense of purpose rekindled.

Even my relationship with Gee seems to take on a lightness.

He's in the shed working on his car. Wrench in hand, and oil rag tucked into his pants.

"What are you working on?" I ask him, I decide it's time to confess it all to him. I had held off for as long as I could, but in the end it was a scab I must pick.

He tells me some things about an alternator, none of which I understand.

"As to that," I pause, " I need to tell you something." It takes all my courage to strum up the words. "I've had a pretty big revelation about money I want to speak to you about."

My words suspend nervously in the air but Gee is no longer paying attention. He is pulling a bolt out beneath the car. "Mmm? What?" he says.

"I am speaking about money babe. I know you don't like it when I talk about it, but I want us to get on the same page."

Gee stops tapping. He puts his wrench down on the floor, covers his face with both hands, makes a sort of groaning noise and massages his eyes. "Oh, God! Not this again," he says.

"Listen, it's not what you think. I firstly want to apologize for accusing you of blocking my money. I know it's not your fault."

He uncovers his eyes, stares into the distance.

"All this time I was frustrated with my business, and I think you were the easy target. The thing is," I fumble with the edge of my shirt, "I don't want to be the one paying for everything anymore. I want you to help contribute."

Gee lets out a sigh of exasperation, "I offered to pay rent and food but you were the one who insisted, telling me you make so much more money than me and yada yada."

"I know! It's just I don't think it's what I want anymore."

"You never know what you want!"

This conversation wasn't going where I'd hoped. I can feel the tinge of defensiveness rise up but I take a deep breath to recalibrate.

"I want us to succeed, to be a team, together."

"Fine with me." He says, picking up his wrench once more.

"Also," I let the words hang and see him flinch. "I haven't been totally honest about my finances. I think a part of me believed you were only with me for my success and competence, so I've been sheltering you from just how bad things have really been."

I tell him everything and Gee listens quietly. His face grim.

There's a part of me that thinks this means the end of our relationship, that he will finally see me for the delusional that

I am but when I finish he simply stands up and cradles me in his arms.

“We will figure it out together.”

“I think I know how,” I say.

“Oh yea?”

“Do you believe in dragons?”

Later that evening, something deep within me comes alive, bubbling to the surface. A flow I had not felt for a long time.

I pick up my laptop and start to write.

16

EMBODIMENT

In 1962 Watson and Crick earned the Nobel Prize for discovering the structure of DNA, the source code to all living life.

Consisting of two long strands that wind around each other in a spiral formation, the double helix structure of DNA is a duality of the feminine and masculine.

In sexual beings, one strand is provided by the father and one by the mother. Two serpents that rise and balance one another. A perfect marriage.

And this duality is reflected inside every cell of our body.

The divine feminine, as we have explored, represents the nonphysical, the unseen and is expressed through thought (conscious or unconscious), imagination, dreams, intuition and intention.

The divine masculine, on the other hand, represents the physical, the seen and is expressed through our actions, words and behaviors.

No one really knows how DNA came about, if it is unique to planet earth (would aliens also have DNA?), and much less is understood about how the two percent difference between the DNA of a human and its closest ape relative has led to the cognitive advancements of the human mind.

But it holds the secret to all physical manifestation—including wealth.

Creation begins first in the seed of thought (nonphysical), which in turn determines our actions and behaviors (physical).

When the two match one another, integrity is achieved and magic unfolds.

When there exists an imbalance, chaos arises to re-establish balance.

Many modern-day manifestation and law of attraction principles would have you believe that all you need is to think positively and that the cornucopia of life will unveil itself to you.

And while it's true that it is possible to manifest purely from the divine feminine (I have often wished for something and then had it come true without lifting a finger), magic is most potent when we acknowledge both physical and nonphysical components.

Intention *and* actions.

Embodiment occurs only when these dual forces come together in unison.

Historically, our society has operated mostly from the divine masculine. The physical world and what science could explain was the truth of what was, and the divine feminine was neglected (even seen as something evil).

Growing up, I—like so many others—was told such things as:

"Money takes hard work."

"You have to sacrifice in order to make money."

"It takes blood, sweat, and tears to make it big."

All of the above are beliefs grounded in the masculine.

Not surprisingly, this became my very experience of making money. Even when I had a huge team and six figure revenue months, I was working myself to the brink of burnout. If I took a holiday with my kids, I always felt guilty—this strange feeling that I always had to be busy, being productive, doing something—lest the house of cards fall down.

Well, it did fall down.

Because I did not understand it takes two to tango.

While science has reduced the world to subatomic particles, calculations and cerebral comforts, many are beginning to understand that the shift away from magical thinking to materialism and scientific advancements is in fact creating even further disenchantment.

Luckily, the world is shifting and awakening to the powers of the divine feminine. Search results for the word "manifestation" have skyrocketed. Law of attraction and even the world of magic are growing in popularity.

Old ways in which we did things no longer seem to apply.

Google search results for the word "manifestation" since 2020. Source, Google.

And we are opening ourselves back up to the power of imagination.

But in this newfound revelation, the divine masculine has become neglected.

The pendulum swinging from one side to the other. Inadvertently creating imbalance, and wrecking more chaos.

Embodiment is a marriage, not one or the other.

When we neglect the divine masculine, we develop apathy to our physical realities.

When we neglect the divine feminine, we make things way harder on ourselves than they need to be.

Many try to root their intentions in greens, but struggle because their actions are in complete contradiction to that which they desire.

When this happens, the dragon breathes flames.

Many try to apply a lot of action to resolve their problems, but struggle because their intentions are driven by reds.

When this happens, the dragon wreaks havoc.

Understanding the dance between the physical and nonphysical is key to embodiment.

And when it feels difficult to establish affinity to money, the divine feminine can be influenced through the intentional intervention of the masculine.

YOU ARE MADE OF STARDUST

Put together by a source code contained within a double helix

Three billion bases, ninety-nine percent of us all the same

A code possessed by all living life on earth

Made up of vibrating atoms that come from exploding stars

With electrons that spin around, just as a moon orbits a planet

The swirl of a galaxy in your eyes

As above so below

Within your cells exists entire universes

All of it occurring, without coercion, without effort

Blood pumping to a heart

A beat of the original drum

You were made in the furnace of the cosmos

You are the story

You are the entire point.

You are made of stardust.

17

MASTER CALLS

Then, this morning, a shift occurred on the astral plane. Easy to miss.

There upon the glades lingered a puddle of lemon sunlight, the first of its kind for some time. A shiver of hope passing through the land. Birds muddling and serenading.

Could it be? Thrills of speculation.

The dryads gather to watch the light breaking against the mountains in thick shafts.

Lumbering downstream, turning behind a curtain of moss, shaking scales, the beast lifts its long majestic neck through the air, letting fall a silver helix of droplets.

The woods and its thousand voices fade to faint.

Huge moths fluttering, wings laced of gold.

Listening, straining tips of roots. Gossip among the dead crowns.

Sniffing the air. There it is again.

Dragon.

Master is calling.

18

THE DIVINE MASCULINE

There's a powerful quote shared by Elizabeth Gilbert in *Eat, Pray, Love* that goes a little something like this:

"A poor man who goes to church every day and prays before the statue of a great saint, begging, "Dear saint-please, please, please...give me the grace to win the lottery." This lament goes on for months. Finally, the exasperated statue comes to life, looks down at the begging man and says in weary disgust, "My son-please, please, please...buy a ticket."

As Gilbert eloquently puts it: Prayer and intention is only half the job. If you desire true transformation then your actions must reflect that which you seek, otherwise all your pleas and desires are boneless, floppy, inert; they swirl at your feet in a cold fog and never lift.

Our actions represent the highest form of manifestation because they reflect back to us the truth of our beliefs, how we are actually engaging the feminine.

You can tell what a person's core beliefs and perspectives are based on how they talk, behave and act.

An insecure person, for instance, behaves and talks differently to a secure one.

It's one thing to affirm yourself that you are wealthy, and to engage the feminine in the greens of abundance and confidence, but if you are avoiding paying your bills or you start complaining about clients being late on payments, this illustrates that in fact the prominent vibration is one of scarcity (red).

It's all well and good to say you feel abundant and to think about abundance, but if you are reacting in fear and panic everytime your bank account goes down, this reveals to you what you truly believe deep down (money is scarce).

It's all well and good to desire millions, but if you spend your time complaining about your dire financial circumstances with your friends, this reveals the truth of your beliefs.

It's all well and good to say you would like to create a great work of art, but if your fingers never lift a brush, you will incite forth chaos.

So long as you engage the divine feminine, continue to desire forward, but do not align your actions, the dragon will spew forth flames to establish balance.

Embodiment is complete only when the masculine of our physical actions mirrors that of the intentions of the feminine.

It's important to point out here that not all action is equal. Forced action is very different to aligned action—action that comes from the core.

When you are forcing yourself to do something, you are acting from a red, not green.

Actions made from reds only result in more of the same.

When you're firing or hiring someone from a space of overwhelm, you will only add more overwhelm to your plate. When you are creating an offer or applying for a job from a space of desperation, you will only attract more scenarios of desperation.

Action also includes non-action. Something that may sound controversial in our day and age where productivity is measured by how busy we keep ourselves. Consequently, it can feel very uncomfortable if we are not always working, always doing something. This leads to busyness for for sake of being busy, which is actually counter-productive.

Procrastination is often a natural protection mechanism to prevent you from going down the wrong rabbit hole. A litmus test for this is to ask yourself if doing the thing would energize or deplete your energy. For example, we may procrastinate exercise but we know we feel better for it afterwards.

This requires an enormous amount of self-awareness. To ignore what our rational mind tells us and instead to tune into the guidance of our intuition.

Deep down in your core you always know when action is forced and when it is inspired. It's easy to tell by the way it *feels.* When actions feel green, they are led by your intuition, when they feel red, they are guided by the rational mind.

This doesn't mean you should not do the things that scare you. Fear, imposter syndrome, and doubt are natural byproducts of stepping into unknowns and, infact, I would argue that if you don't feel a little bit afraid, you aren't really growing. Our greatest gifts to the world are always our biggest shadows. Fear is always an invitation to transmute to courage.

And the things that make you feel most like an imposter are always your greatest portals of receiving. For instance, my gift to this world is teaching and writing, these activities place me in my biggest greens, but they also place me into my deepest reds, I have the most doubt over these creations.

Only aligned action can help you to overstep these reds. Forced action driven from the rational mind can never truly overcome fear and doubt.

Aligning actions also doesn't necessarily mean spending money. Most of the desires we have include many steps prior to a financial outlay.

For example, if you desire to invest into stocks, you would first need to understand which stocks to purchase, how the market works, perhaps even join groups involving discussions around trading. These are all actions that signal the intent and do not actually cost anything.

Consider the desires you established in earlier chapters. And then consider your own actions and behaviors in relation to these steps.

If you desire more freedom in your business, are you yourself intentionally prying back more time in your schedule or do you continue to work through endless to-do lists day in and day out?

If you desire to purchase a new home, are you actively searching for these homes, reaching out to realtors and visiting them, or are you holding conditions over your actions of: "When I have more money, then I can start looking for homes"?

If you desire to host retreats or an event, are you actively and intentionally looking for venues and putting feelers out or, again, do your actions and behaviors simply keep you in the same loop of where you are?

If you desire to travel, are you actively searching out destinations and looking at flights?

If you desire a new car, are you actively test-driving options?

The most powerful way to influence the divine feminine and imprint upon the subconscious is to intentionally shift our actions towards that which we intend for ourselves.

And how we spend and receive money is no exception.

Spend in Green

Consider the ways in which you make payments, how you pay your bills. Are you frustrated that you have to pay your power company? Do you feel angry that the government requires taxes from you?

Most of us, when we pay our bills or spend money, do so from a space of lack or frustration. We think about the money leaving our bank accounts and that is all we focus on.

We take money out at the ATM and feel ourselves punched to the gut. We dread opening our bank accounts for fear of the burning shame that comes from seeing pitiful figures.

How we spend our money, how we allow outflows to occur, is a crucial part of how we engage the divine masculine and in turn how we cultivate financial freedom.

One should avoid paying invoices or bills until they are in a space of gratitude or green about it.

The way that I do this is I usually bulk invoice payments to one day of the week. Before I sit down to pay those I owe, I make sure to get myself into a good feeling space. Sometimes this means I will go exercise, or paint, or spend time with friends or meditate.

I will then sit down and say a heartfelt 'thank you' for the invoice paid, taking a moment to appreciate the services I received in exchange for this payment and to appreciate my dragon for allowing me to experience such things.

Even debt repayments, something that many people despise, should be done from this space of gratitude. Because every debt represents a value exchange. You agreed to borrow money (what a luxury that someone would agree to lend you money) and did so because you saw value in doing so.

To then resent those who loaned you the money, or interest rates, is in direct contradiction of what you desire—prosperity. For the version of yourself who embodies prosperity would not belittle or scorn those who helped them rise to such a position.

The version of yourself that is abundant and enjoying the fruits of wealth would not resent outflows of cash, they would not default on payments, they would not pay their staff begrudgingly.

Even if you cannot pay someone back because you do not have the money, it is very important that you open a communication line with that individual or company and start making small repayments, even if it's just a few dollars so that you can create integrity with that which you desire.

I have a friend who owes a substantial amount of money to creditors. They have big aspirations, to earn millions of dollars, but refuse to pay back all the money they owe. One day, while having lunch, this friend proceeded to inform me that they intended to write a letter to all those they owed informing them that they had not been of sound mind and that it was the creditor's fault for even lending them money. Not only does this type of action directly enchant that very reality (of supposed insanity) into existence, but it contradicts the intended desires. So long as they refuse to pay back the sums loaned, they will continue to struggle to attract and receive money for their actions are out of integrity with the feminine.

When you go to the grocery store and you swipe your card at checkout, feel deep gratitude for the outflow of money, spend it in green.

When you pay for gas at the station, do so appreciating how amazing it is that you get to fuel your car for another week.

When you get letters in the mail and you put them on your counter and they collect dust because you're too afraid to open them, what are these actions telling you about what you truly believe about money?

Remember, the dragon cannot contradict your own actions. If you spend money in red, yet continue to desire for bigger, better things, you will incite flames forth.

Money is purely imagined; it will come and it will go.

It is here not to serve the purpose of collecting dust in some great tank you will dive into, but to be used to expand your experiences in life. It is meant to be spent and enjoyed, we cannot, afterall, take money with us to the grave.

You must not only get comfortable with outflows but you must feel gratitude for them for every outflow represents an exchange of value and value is what motivates you forward.

Let it go. Let it go.

And let it go with gratitude and trust, then watch what happens. It will come back tenfold.

If you're trying to buy something online, or pay for services, or pay for a new mentor, don't pay when you're in red. Wait until you feel green and then push buy.

One of my ethos in my company is to tell prospective buyers to never purchase from me when they are in red. What I have found through the years in working with people is that those people who invest in me while they were in a red state are usually very needy and it doesn't usually end well.

On the flipside, clients who invest while they feel in flow, excited, or grateful experience the most transformative shifts with very little effort. They understand that the outflow is a way to send a clear signal of their intentions, and always the dragon returns it.

Again, think about your money in the context of a friendly dragon that wishes to please, or any relationship for that matter.

If you got upset every time your partner left your sight, if it panicked you, this would not lead to a very healthy relationship but rather one of codependency that would likely end in tears.

By getting upset every time your dragon or partner walks out the door, what you are signaling is that you do not believe they are trustworthy, that you do not believe you are good enough or that they will return.

Just as you must hold trust that your partner will return to you, the same rules apply to money.

Even if that means you have to put your bum under the sun for half an hour, do that. Find what activities help you get back into good feeling states and build up your toolbox, we are each unique and what will work for some may not work for you. Go explore. Go date yourself. It'll be the most fulfilling thing you'll ever do in your life.

If you don't know what gets you in green, that's probably the reason you don't have the money that you want. And if it feels impossible to get into green for a potential purchase, it's probably not meant for you.

Not only should you ensure you spend money from a green but you should also actively look to spend towards those things that you desire.

So many times in my life I have wanted something that technically didn't make financial sense on paper.

When I decided to book the photoshoot, this didn't make any rational or financial sense. But it was compelling to me, it felt like fun and play.

This doesn't mean you have to go and make yourself bankrupt or spend all your money to the point where you are in deep anxiety. There are ways to spend in small ways that still align actions to intentions.

For example, if you are looking to renovate your house, purchase tile samples.

If you are looking to travel abroad, purchase one of the tours you'd like to do. If you cannot afford this, then start reaching out to tour providers and enquiring.

If you are looking to hire a private mentor, purchase one of their lower cost courses, or join the groups they host.

Make sure that what you spend money on isn't to escape a red, but rather motivated by an expansion in greens. Again, ask yourself: "Would this energize or deplete me of energy?".

The way we spend money is a powerful way to stretch ourselves to new income brackets and to compel belief towards that which we desire.

When we are intentional in shifting our actions, we foster integrity between the feminine and the masculine, and achieve embodiment.

ATM EXERCISE

This exercise will test the limits of your trust with money, but in a way that is relatively low risk.

Please note—at time of writing it is still possible to take out cash although the world is on the cusp of another metamorphosis and soon money will likely be all digital. If this is the case, you can still perform this exercise by shifting your digital money into a separate account instead of withdrawing it at an ATM.

How to Do

Go to an ATM and take out a sum of money that stretches you. This could be $20 if you only have $50 in your account or it could be a few thousand dollars if you have a larger chunk.

The amount you take out is subjective to you and how much you have in your account.

What you want is a figure that at first makes you slightly panic or freak out. Because this exercise is about transmuting that red and trusting. It is an exercise I do whenever I'm feeling myself falling back into scarcity or financial reds.

It's so powerful because it is literally putting you into that energetic space of, "I trust money is coming back."

Once withdrawn, you're not going to spend that money. You're just going to put it in your wallet and that's it.

You're not going to use it. The money's still there. So it's not like I'm telling you to go give it to somebody and squander it somewhere. You still have the money, technically, but it's not in your account, so it's not functioning dollars.

One of the things I like to do with this exercise is—let's say I take out $2,000—and I'm walking down the street and I see things that I like, I go: "Ah, I can buy that because I have $2,000 in my pocket right now. I could buy that. I could buy that. I could buy that. I could buy that. I could buy that." So I buy things in my head with that money, over and over again.

Usually, I end up forgetting about the money. Two or three weeks later, I totally forget the money is there, and it's the most delicious surprise when I remember it or find it stashed somewhere.

If you find yourself standing in front of the ATM and you're thinking, "I'm not doing this exercise. This is stupid. I don't want to take this money out. I really need it," take a moment to get back into green. Do not attempt this while you are in red.

Remind yourself that you will still be in possession of the money.

And foster the courage to trust your dragon.

Receiving Money

Our ability to compound wealth depends largely on the way in which we receive money itself.

Again, if you pay attention to the way in which you react to money coming into your life, you'll likely find that it is also done in red.

It's either too small a sum and you feel dissatisfied.

Or the sum scares you, and fears arise.

How we receive money is a big part of how we engage the divine masculine, and can help us to remove conditions over our greens.

The thing that I struggled with for the longest time was receiving testimonials and people saying nice things about me. People would send me testimonials or messages of their success and I would feel uncomfortable. Unsurprisingly, I began to receive fewer and fewer of these until I learned to fully embrace these and receive them in gratitude.

When we are afraid of receiving or ungrateful in receiving, we prevent ourselves from receiving more of that which we desire.

Many of us have leaky beliefs when it comes to who and what constitutes deserving of money.

I have a friend who feels shame because much of the money in her life comes not from her own hard work and sacrifice but rather from an inheritance. So long as she carries shame and acts in shame around this, she prevents herself from receiving at the full capacity.

A prevalent belief that can prevent many of us from receiving money is the one where it doesn't feel fair to do so, especially when so many others are without.

Many of us were raised with the ethos of: "If Sarah can't have one, no one can." And while this value illustrates that there is care and consideration for others it can lead to people-pleasing and ultimately helps no one.

Consider this, if you're driving to a location and someone in the passenger seat tells you all the directions, or a GPS does it for you—do you actually remember or learn how to get to this location on your own? Likely not. Until you figure it out on your own, the directions will never click.

And while we like to believe that giving to others to help them avoid their own struggles is an act of kindness, truthfully it is an act of selfishness, because you deprive the individual from having their own "ah ha" moment, you prevent them from the experience of growth.

I'm not suggesting that altruism or charity should be thrown out the door, on the contrary, what I mean is that you will have a far greater impact helping others if you have money behind you. Preventing yourself from receiving because others do not does nothing for no one.

If you are going to give, make sure it's not driven by guilt. There's a lot of: "You need to give generously if you make money" ideologies that can actually trap us into feast to famine cycles and prevent us from receiving.

Back in 2022 I had a friend ask me for a substantial sum of money as a loan. In my gut I didn't want to lend the money but this made me feel guilty. What proceeded was that I unconsciously drove my revenues right down, which then allowed me to say "no" without feeling the guilt purely as I didn't have it, but it was a really messed up way of going about it.

Remember, money is imagined, which means it is infinite (as there exists no bounds to human imagination), which also means that another's success never minimizes your own. And vice versa. The best way to create a better world for others, is to create a better world for yourself.

One of the little things I do in my business that helps me to find a genuine space of celebration for money coming into my life is to set up a phone notification where I receive a text every time I make a sale. I include little party and dragon emojis in the text to remind me to find a space of celebration and gratitude.

I also employ a magical technique called invocation to achieve much the same thing.

Invocation is the practice of placing another's perspective into your own nervous system. Seeing the world through a different lens essentially. I'll often invoke fictional characters, historic personas, and even animals—there is no right or wrong way to do it but you want to find a perspective that will be useful to you and what you aim to achieve.

I love invoking Cleopatra for she was an alchemist and the wealthiest human of her time. I'll walk down the sidewalk and bring her perspective into my own nervous system, my shoulders will go back, I stand a little taller, I'm calm and serene around money knowing that I own coffers of gold.

Another fun invocation exercise I like to employ when I find a dime or dollar on the street is to pretend I'm a Middle Age peasant. I'll pick it up as if I had just discovered a fortune, a king's ransom and treasure the dollar.

If you pay attention to wealthy people you will see that they hold a great amount of respect for all money—big sums and small. Kim Kardahsian, a billionaire, once joked that she gets so excited every time she finds $20 in her winter jacket.

When we can find gratitude for even the smallest sums, it compounds our ability to receive more.

Create your own ritual around celebrating money coming in.

Perhaps you sound a tuning fork each time you receive money or ring a singing bowl. Maybe you have a special dance, maybe a special handshake you do with yourself. Whatever it is, find some way to celebrate the bounty of your dragon.

The more you do this, the more your dragon will bring you.

CREATING A MONEY MAP

A Money Map is a powerful way to celebrate the money you receive and invite more in. I learned this exercise from one of my early mentors Jesse Elder.

Essentially, you create a grid for all the days of the month.

I like to do this on a whiteboard and I will keep the board somewhere in plain view in my home.

How to Do

Write down your money objective (MO) for the month at the top of the board. If you are not yet in affinity with money (red) then make your MO an amount you would normally make in a month. If you are in affinity with money (green) then stretch yourself and choose a sum that still feels believable but that is beyond what you currently earn.

Insert all the guaranteed sums of money that you know will come in under the appropriate days. For example, if you earn a paycheck and you get paid $800 every week on a Thursday, you would write $800 down under each Thursday of the month. If you have clients on recurrent payment plans, then enter those sums under the corresponding days that payments will go through.

Only write down the money you know will come in, not anticipated, not hoped for, not potential, but guaranteed.

Subtract the total sum of incoming money from your MO.

You now have your gap-to-go (G2G). Write this out below your MO.

Every time more money comes into your life, no matter how big or small, write it down in your graph and adjust your G2G.

Be sure to take a moment to celebrate the figures received and to thank your dragon.

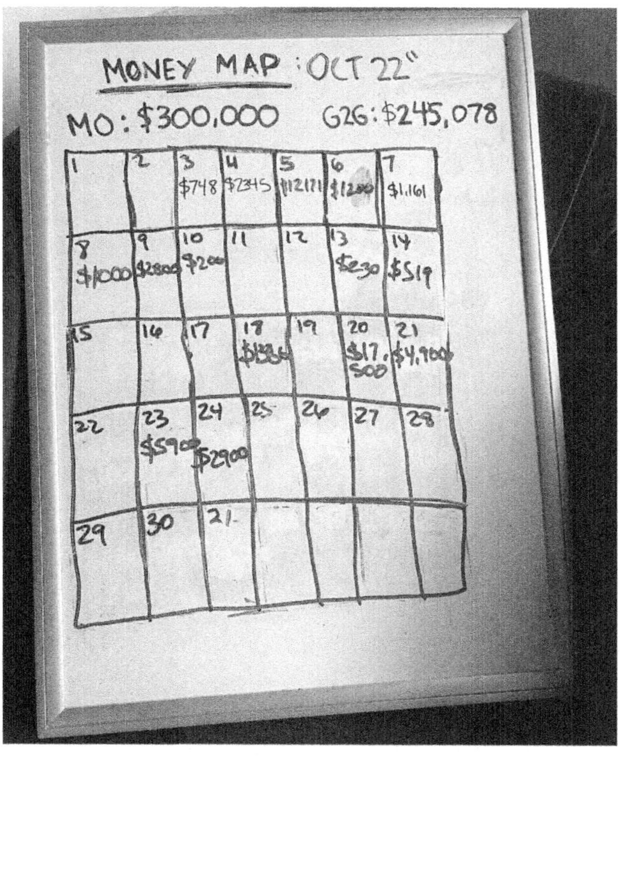

19

MASTER VISITS

Master visits.

Have you heard?

Here. Now.

The dryads whisper sweet-nectared words.

Dragon arcs high in the sky, its scales shimmering blue.

Spotting Master along the ridge of the enchanted forest, the great beast tumbles downwards across the lake, its reflection quivering across the water.

Water. Air. Water.

Enveloping Master in a whoosh, Dragon curls its long serpentine tail against Master's cheeks. The heat of a body, the pulse of a vein. The velvet of possibility.

Master laughs, the beast purrs and the wood pigeons chorus.

Bluebell haze, opal sky, dawdling glades, Dragon's scales once more bejeweled. Tiny droplets, as if perspiring.

A tinkle, a sequined shiver, the dryads come flirting.

Master has returned.

Sweet sighs.

There is hope for love, joy, and play.

"What has happened here?" Master asks, eyes scanning across a parched land. The scent of the earth, fungal spores, through sleeping trees.

It was Dragon. The dryads cannot help but gossip.

"I have abandoned you great beast, no more."

Exposing a belly, Dragon coos. Bulbous yellow eyes staring back absurdly.

The fields are calmer today than they were yesterday, rhizomes offering but a low crackle, chords of content.

Swallows cut through the air like blue scissors.

A sweet, sweet breeze blows through the forest, lifting the grass along the hill. Above, an immense sky. Like a painting, subtle graduations of pink, yellow, and blue to mimic the progression of an aria, as if it were formulated from a sheet of music.

Grasshoppers spring forth.

The crunch of a leaf inside the mouth of a caterpillar.

Master's thoughts no longer taste like metal. No longer molten hot.

Tongue slithering and low-lashed glances. Dragon smiles like the frogs.

Master is here.

20

A MATTER OF INTEGRITY

"You can will yourself into action, but you cannot will yourself into will" - Einstein

While, in principle, embodiment—to feel and act positively around money—is simple enough, often we may encounter times where it feels very difficult to think and act green around our money.

Even though we understand the implications of not doing so, even though we desire to do so, the will to embody affinity with money may feel out of reach.

When this occurs, usually it's a signal that there is an integrity issue elsewhere in our lives. Integrity as in the masculine no longer matches the feminine.

This could be personal relationships, a career, friendships, even our own wellbeing.

Because money is a figment of the human imagination, yet one that has far-reaching implications in our daily lives, it is one of the easiest mechanisms of chaos for us to catalyze transformation in our own lives.

In other words, if there are areas in your life that are not aligned, oftentimes, we will use money as a way to signal this misalignment.

For example, I once spoke to someone who struggled to sell her home, which had been on the market for over two years. She was separating from her husband, who was a major emotional trigger for her, but because the home was not selling, she was still living with him. When we spoke, she told me such things as "When the home sells and the money comes in, then I can be happy and independent." She was struggling to feel inspired about potential jobs or creative opportunities and it was even harder for her to feel affinity towards money. My advice to her was to move out as soon as possible, to align her actions in the direction of her greens. I told her to go live with a friend or family, or find an Airbnb, anything to establish integrity. She took a leap of faith, fostered some courage, and took my advice. Within three weeks the home sold. Not only that, but a month after she took the leap, she found herself excited about potential business ideas and creative pursuits that had eluded her for so long.

When there are dynamics in our life that are out of alignment, it will feel difficult to establish embodiment of our greens and we will often use money as a way to signal this misalignment.

While it seems crude, and even disturbing to think that we may be the ones inviting chaos purposely into our lives, the truth is that chaos is one of the most powerful ways to encourage growth.

Think about all the biggest expansions you yourself have come to experience; likely these came on the back of not so pleasant experiences.

Getting fired from your job, losing your clients, being dumped.

While these events, in the moment, are painful, with the grace of time we often look back with gratitude for them for they were the moments that shifted us into something far greater.

If it had not been for the botched surgery I experienced years ago, likely I would still be obsessing with plastic surgery.

Chaos plays the role of re-establishing balance. When the dragon burns your world to flames, it is only because it desires to serve you, to bring you to that which you seek. Always, chaos is a sign of conditions existing over our greens, always it signals transformation in action.

Much of the financial chaos I came to face was the result of me not creating in the direction of my desires (to publish a book) and feeling trapped in my relationship. Deep down I believed that Gee was with me for the money, a belief that contradicted what I truly desired for myself. I found it difficult to find affinity with my money, to think positively about it, simply because I was not allowing myself to receive so long as old structures remained in place.

The main dynamics of our life include: the relationship we hold with ourselves, our children and spouse (or partners), our family, friends & peers, our work or business, and society as a whole. If we are experiencing contradictory reds in anyone one of these, embodiment of abundance will feel difficult.

One of the first things I tend to ask entrepreneurs or artists who are facing financial plateaus is: do you feel inspired by what you're creating? Usually financial stagnation is a signal that the core has moved on, but the rational mind is keeping you in the same circuits and structures.

If you are unhappy in your job, relationship, body, or business it's likely all sorts of financial chaos will arise. Unexpected bills, cars breaking down, etc.

While it's true that there are many successful individuals who are in unhappy marriages, or who hate their bodies, in general, success is harder to come by if you are feeling stuck in your personal life.

Again, the reason for this is simply because money is one of the easiest ways for us to communicate misalignment.

Far easier, and with far less implications than say—using our health (if you are experiencing health issues, the same applies, you are signaling to yourself misalignment).

It's important you remember there exists no conditions over wealth other than embodying affinity towards money. I do not want to encourage you to enter a witch hunt where you try to shift the blame to others, this will only lead you further astray.

But in the instance where you genuinely try to feel green about money, yet cannot get there, then likely it is because you are employing your dragon to burn down those things in your life that no longer serve you.

If you have been finding it very difficult to feel and think positively about your money, then ask yourself where in your life you are currently feeling trapped.

Trapped is the polar opposite of freedom, and the desire for more money is usually one that boils down to freedom.

Perhaps you hate the job you're in, perhaps you don't like your spouse very much, maybe you are overwhelmed or feeling stuck in your business or with an offer you are creating.

Perhaps you have an addiction that you feel you cannot escape.

If there is something that immediately comes to mind, then chances are this is the thing stopping you from obtaining embodiment.

The key here is to first try and transmute that dynamic.

For example, if you feel stuck in your relationship, Then see if you can transmute this to feeling free and grateful. Focus on all the positive things about the relationship or of your partner. Write out lists of what you *do want.* Often this exercise will elicit an immediate shift in the parties involved.

If you hate yourself for vaping, then shift the perspective where it's no longer a trigger. Accept yourself as you are, vaper and all.

If it's not possible to do, then you are clearly telling yourself to change behaviors and actions around it. To show up differently.

When we dream big things for ourselves, this ultimately means we will outgrow current structures or relationships.

Letting go of those circumstances or things that no longer work for us is always the hardest part.

Remember, you still get to receive from your dragon even when different areas of your life don't feel aligned, none of these are ever conditions to wealth.

Even if you lack purpose and direction, even if you are grumpy or sad or heartbroken—your dragon can still deliver.

But if it feels like it's not possible to find affinity, then you must foster courage in other areas in order to reach the greens.

EXERCISE: IDENTIFY THE TRIGGERS

When I was in the deep end of depression in my previous business, I started to chart my emotions on a graph, and this technique really helped to pull me out of the reds.

Each day, I would average out my emotional state and plot it on the chart (I talk about this in more depth inside Magic Source Codes).

This method works really well to help you develop emotional intelligence (the first step to being able to transmute reds to greens).

You can take it one step further by listing out all the things you did that day, or the people you encountered, to help you identify triggers that may exist outside of your conscious realm.

I used this exercise not long ago and it became clear at once that every time I smoked weed I fell into reds. I guess I had been in denial of this before, I even believed that weed helped with my creativity, but seeing it charted out made it clear as day. I haven't smoked since, and my money has reflected this too.

If you discover that hanging around certain people, or doing certain things pulls you out of your greens, depletes you of energy, then see if you can pattern interrupt the dynamic.

Again, it's important to remember that money doesn't care if you smoke weed or hang around people that complain all day, but if you are actively engaged in situations or environments that no longer serve you, there's a high chance you will use money as a mechanism of chaos to elicit change.

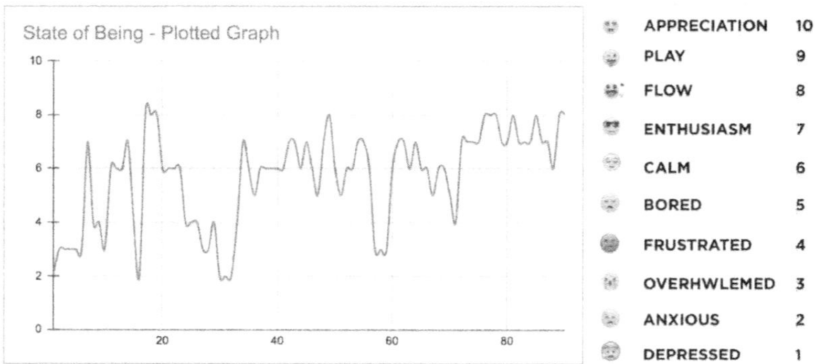

21

MONEY ALTAR

The words have been pouring out.

I'm not even sure how it's happening but ever since picking up my laptop, I have not stopped writing. I'm not doing it for the money, or because I even expect to complete a book, but because it is a compulsion of my core.

Each day I sit across the sofa, fingers tapping away in a flurry. From this vantage point, I notice that a sliver of light shines across one of the clay snakes (which really looks like a dragon) atop the mantle at the same time every day. A precise astronomical measurement for anyone who pays close enough attention.

Before I even have a finished manuscript, I decide to update my social media profile bios to say "author". I create a sales page and begin pre-selling copies of my book, which I title: Magic Source Codes, and magically sell over one hundred.

My whole life I had aspired to become a published author.

And while I had attempted hundreds of times, deleting and rewriting various stories, nothing had stuck.

And now, as if by some miracle, in less than two weeks, my first book is written.

All because I found affinity to money. I wrote, I embodied (by declaring myself the author, making payments towards invoices owed, and fostering courage to change structures that no longer served me), and I trusted through the chaos.

I retire the lists of culprits. I stop looking for problems. Instead, I write gratitude lists of all the ways that my dragon has enriched my life. I sing its praises; I tickle it blue.

As if a cork is undone, money starts to flow in more steadily. Leads and clients begin to enquire about working with me.

The potential contract issue that could have set me back $200,000 has been absolved. A great weight lifted.

What's more, I receive a tax rebate, in the sum totaling the amount owed from my last company.

It makes me laugh.

Here I had been all along feeling resentful for the mess I had led myself in in my pursuit of wealth, getting triggered and jealous by those who succeeded around me, warning anyone who would listen of the perils of loving money over wellbeing.

Meanwhile, behind the scenes I was clearly yearning for more because I was comparing myself and feeling frustrated in my progress.

Believing money was to blame for my problems had been the problem. Believing I was stuck in existing structures, was what had kept me stuck financially.

It had nothing to do with Gee, or the economy, or the strategies I employed.

Feeling red about my money, and not having the courage to create in the unknown, had been the flames all along.

When I was making millions in my last company, none of it had made sense on paper. The cash had rushed in so fast I could barely keep up.

When people would ask me how I had done it I would always respond with, "Honestly, I don't know."

This version of myself was not comparing herself, she was not frustrated by money. She was not trying to heal money blocks.

She did not place chains on her dragon, she reveled in its glory. She let it come and go, without going into red about it. Every dollar that came in, no matter how big or small, was cause to celebrate. She created from flow, from her core, and from play.

The world was abundant, and I, perceptive to it.

That was how and why I had made the numbers I had hit.

That magical kind of money.

HONORING REST AND RECOVERY

Through the years, I've come to experience creativity manifest itself as seasons.

Periods when I am deeply compelled by a vision, and moments when it all but dries up.

Cycles when revenues come pouring in, and others where it plateaus or even goes downhill.

There is a false notion out there that success can only look like an upward line of affluence.

When in reality, all systems in nature observe rest and recovery phases.

We tend to be resistant to these periods, they feel uncomfortable, and society typically frowns upon anything that doesn't outwardly look like growth.

But rest precedes expansion. And a cocoon phase means transformation.

Sometimes these moments last a few days, months or even years.

The greatest struggle comes from our own minds, how we believe there is something wrong. How we think we have failed.

Being at war with our circumstances only distends the time to get there.

Creative blocks are never a problem.

For they serve introspection, alignment, and energy for the growth to come.

Don't fight them, don't chastise yourself for them.

Rather surrender. Go inwards, go into the other (non-business-related activities) that put you in greens.

Tides come in and go out, just as the butterfly turns to jelly to become a monarch.

Remember—regardless which phase you're in—your dragon is still eager to serve you.

22

FINDING COURAGE

When there is no anxiety to reach a particular destination, there is an opportunity for adventure. - Lyanda Lynn Haupt

Deep within your soul, lies a creative impulse to expand your greens.

A story waiting to be told.

Perhaps you are a musician who aspires to create worlds of sound.

Perhaps you are an artist who desires to create worlds of color.

Perhaps you are a business person who desires to solve big problems.

Perhaps you are in a stage where you don't really know what you desire to create.

In all cases, the impulse is to believe that the end outcome of our creations is what we aspire for.

Society tells us that purpose is about a long-term goal, a profession or vocation we choose, and that money is a result of having a clear vision.

When really, it's the process of turning a dream into a reality which captivates the human spirit.

The envisioned outcome is simply a target that gives us the direction and motivation to start creating.

When we create, we ourselves become transformed through the process and grow into deeper levels of mastery.

Unfortunately, the focus on money as the end game often leads to a situation where the authentic expression and love for the craft take the back seat, while we hustle to figure out how to grow our fanbase and our finances.

We start doing things for popularity rather than purpose. Putting us on the fast-track to burnout and anxiety and extending the time it takes to get where we seek.

The dream is never about the outcome itself, it's never about the house or fancy trips or the finished manuscript, rather it is an expansion in our greens. This is what compels the soul.

And the joy is in the journey, not the destination. Savoring the present moment and giving ourselves the greens in the here and now is how we speed up manifestations.

Money doesn't care if you have clarity around your niche, occupation, or trade. It doesn't care if you have a six-step business plan. These are not conditions to wealth. Again, you can find ample examples of individuals who lack purpose in the traditional sense yet have a lot of money.

When we make creation about accomplishing a certain thing, or seeking validation for what we do, we lead ourselves astray. We create conditions over the greens.

When we create purely from a space of greens (which sometimes means taking no action and honoring rest and recovery), and hold affinity towards our dragons, suddenly we become magnets to others and our desires.

Embodiment of these greens is our purpose here.

To feel, think, behave, act and speak as if it already were.

The perfect marriage between the divine feminine and masculine.

This is the alchemy of financial freedom.

To act abundant even if we are broke.

To take the leap when we have no idea how it will work out.

To follow our soul's calling when all the odds are stacked up against us.

To make the investment even when our rational mind tells us otherwise.

To create the things that compel us even if it makes no rational sense.

Of course, this requires no short amount of courage.

Courage is a vibration of play. One of the highest alchemy

states.

Mammals come into this earth embodying play. Babies, puppies, lambs. For it is through play that we come to learn how to navigate our world and deepen social bonds.

As Stuart Brown, scientist and author of "*Play: How It Shapes the Brain, Opens the Imagination, and Invigorates the Soul*" once said: "Play seems to be one of the most advanced methods nature has invented to allow a complex brain to create itself".

It allows us to overcome fears and step forward into the unknown. It is a mixture of inquisitiveness, spontaneity, and courage. When we bungee jump off a bridge, it is thanks to the vibration of play. When we create *despite* past failures, this is also a form of play.

One of the easiest ways to tap into this powerful creative state is to seek out things outside of your comfort zone.

If you know you are out of integrity in one area of your life; perhaps you hate the job you're in but stay because you're afraid of how you're going to pay the bills, maybe you want to make a big pivot in your business but you're anxious of how it will be received, and if the fear is too great to align intentions to actions, start in small ways in other areas of your life.

Find things that feel a little bit scary but also compulsive and exciting for you to do. Things that energize you. For example, perhaps you have always wanted to try a type of dancing but you never did because you're scared you'll embarrass yourself. Maybe you want to approach someone from the opposite (or same sex), but again the potential rejection has always prevented you.

Courage and play are vibrations that we build within ourselves first and foremost. If we cannot face the big elephant in the room we can seek out this vibration in smaller ways, and this will naturally overspill. If you continue to seek out play, you will soon enough find the courage to make the moves that need to be made to align the feminine and masculine.

Releasing shame is another powerful way to tap into play.

Coming out as a witch on my public profile required a lot of courage. I believed that people would shun me, ridicule me and that my business would suffer. When in actual fact, the opposite happened, my business grew, revenues climbed and I realigned.

Many times throughout my life I have carried shame around the way that I operate and create.

My desires and passions have often been felt with deep flow and compulsion. And then, sometimes quite suddenly, just dry up.

I have often chastised myself for this, felt guilty and like I was doing something wrong.

Outwardly looking in this kind of behavior is usually classed as or associated with ADHD, it's seen as a problem, something to be fixed.

But in feeling guilty or shame for outgrowing my shell, I always ultimately trapped myself, preventing that which I really wanted from being received.

And every time I have tried to force against it, rationalise my way into just sucking it up, it's always brought in more chaos.

Giving myself permission to flow where compulsion goes has been something I've had to work really hard to teach myself.

Understanding that it always costs me more when I don't, has been a lesson I've had to learn many times before.

Shame is the belief that we are not good enough, it is a renouncement of our duality.

But play is imperfect (infact it can look quite chaotic).

Just as we all are.

And accepting this duality, is what creates true authenticity.

Unfortunately, it took me to almost lose it all for me to no longer care what others might think.

When I finally made the pivot in my business, things started to flow again financially. My flow restored itself. The author, a deep lifelong desire of mine, finally pierced through.

One way to release shame is to confess it in a safe group environment. The Catholic rite of confessionals is a testament to the power of this exercise.

Come clean about your shame to those who it involves, to close friends or peers you trust and you will feel—almost instantly—a great weight lifted.

Again, if you cannot find the courage to do this, seek out courage by doing things outside of your comfort zone first.

It is much easier for you to allow yourself to receive, to believe you are worthy, without the chains of shame tethered on. It is much easier to create embodiment when we are leading the way with play.

Play also means following the beat of your own drum.

Often, we try to mimic strategies we see others succeed with, we force ourselves to fit into molds that do not belong to us.

A year ago, I shifted my business model to one I saw my mentor use. She was making millions per month and I believed this was the key to my own success. Inadvertently, I soon found myself uninspired and unfulfilled. Trapped. Which had the opposite effect on my revenues.

There is no such thing as "one size fits all" when it comes to making money.

Honoring our greens is all that is required and this will look different to everyone.

Everything and anything can work, so long as you lead the way with your greens.

YOU ARE WHO YOU HANG AROUND

The myths of money you have come to adopt in your own life are likely the result of the tales told by those closest to you.

In modern times, the phrase "you are who you hang around" has become a common way of expressing the idea that our social environment can have a powerful impact on who we are and who we become.

If your group of friends tends to struggle with addiction, chances are you will too. If your group of friends excels at a particular subject or holds a certain belief, you will likely absorb this as well.

Our desire to fit in overrides any financial desire and one of the easiest and arguably fastest ways to elicit a shift in perspectives is to intentionally seek out those who tell the tales of money you wish to share in.

If you have family or friends that are constantly in red or speaking of money in red, try to remove yourself from them for a little while—at least until you feel confident in your new narrative. Again, this may require courage for you to stand your ground and set boundaries so actively seek out play in your life.

Sometimes we may not directly have access to the connections or people that are more in line with our desires but we can call for help to be guided towards and to receive these.

Set the intention to attract those who have affinity to money into your life and they will come to you.

Align the masculine by actively seeking out these communities and you will accelerate results.

If you need inspiration feel free to join the private Money Magic group on Facebook.

23

DRAGON

The serpent is a descendant of the dragon.

Wrap its tail in its mouth and it is the symbol of infinity.

Humans do not see dragons, not the way dragons see.

Flesh puckered in pores, starfish mouths and blind as a moles. Pupils that glint to the sky. Fingers that grab. Humans forget the commands. They live in a world of Maya.

They forget that diamonds are forged in the heat of inferno.

They forget that burned canopies are what allow the sunlight to come through, making way for new growth.

So Dragon lurked, watching, curling and pruning. Spitting forth its flames.

Because Dragon is a creature of balance.

Flames or treasure, it makes no odds. Both are in its nature.

Now, gone are the days of blood and gore. Of cages and dissonance.

On the astral plane, Master commands treasure forth.

Where fields of charred flowers lay to waste, new shoots of lavender spring forth. Inside the purple petals are tiny jewels that wink to the suns.

Clouds that were once black and scudded, roll cotton candy pink in the sky.

The rain of acid stops.

A rumble in the belly.

Preening, sleeping.

There is hope. There is hope.

Emeralds that shine green as a beetle's carapace.

Fire in the throat. Steady, holding, dissipating.

Master once cast Dragon to the shadows.

But now Master knows.

That Dragon is ever loyal.

24

HOW TO TRAIN YOUR DRAGON

"The true dragon is a creature of such refinement of spirit that they can only take on form in this world if they are conceived by the most skilled imagination. And even then, the said imagination must be in some place heavily impregnated with magic, which helps to weaken the walls between the world of the seen and unseen." - *Terry Pratchett*

In one of the oldest surviving English literary works, the famous poem *Beowulf*, the protagonist is a wise and respected ruler who confronts a dragon hoarding treasure at the cost of his own life.

The dragon becomes angered when a thief awakens it and takes a valuable item. In its rage, the dragon embarks on a campaign of destruction, burning down villages and wreaking havoc on the countryside.

In reference to the myth Kathryn Hume writes:

Whether giant or dwarf, dragon or draugr, the supernatural creatures function as foils for the hero, and in the sagas, the hero's confrontation of the monster exists to test the protagonist and to affirm his status as professional hero.

Beowulf's dragon represents the chaotic and destructive forces that challenge the stability and order of human society. It embodies the inevitability of mortality and the struggle against the unknown.

In much the same way that the dragon breathes fire into the world, seemingly preying on society, and allowing the hero to put his or her strength to the service of others, so too does money.

Both savior and foe.

Long before European folklore hit the scene, dragons were imagined mostly as divine creatures of abundance and protection.

These were the stories we told.

But somewhere along the lines, the tales changed.

And became one of greed, evil, dissonance and flames.
Greedy Smaug atop his pile of treasure.

Reflecting back to us our own misinterpretation.

We are a people at war with money.

Its myth turned into one of great chaos and despair.

But the Dragon is neither good or bad. It is merely the mirror of our own expression. It exists purely as our own test of heroism. Our willingness to step boldly towards unknowns.

If we go to war with it, it is with ourselves that we fight.

For money is but a figment of the imagination. The money in our bank accounts, a direct reflection of our own integrity with it.

It is in the cusp of imagination that prosperity and wealth are created. And in order to manifest these into the physical, we must manifest these intentions through our own bodies.

Embodiment, and nothing else, is required for success.

The marriage of the divine feminine and masculine.

If you are angry, bitter or resentful of money, your dragon will bring to you more flames to stoke these embers. You will experience and perceive more reasons why money is the root of all problems and will prevent yourself from receiving.

If you are shaming others for possessing that which you do not have, but behind closed doors are engaging the feminine in your desires for more, your dragon will belch out lava.

Thinking positively about money is only half of the equation.

Our words, how we act and behave completes the double helix.

Be impeccable with your word, do not complain or speak about your financial woes unless it is in the context of releasing shame.

Be impeccable with your actions and behaviors, do not allow yourself to remain in relationships or circumstances where you feel trapped or confused.

Intentionally take actions to mirror your intentions.

Even if your world feels like it's being burned to flames right now, trust that from the ashes the phoenix will rise.

Step boldly forward, a hero emboldened in courage.

Love your dragon, and act like you do.

These are the commands of the money dragon.

DON'T GIVE UP ON YOU

As you begin to follow the things that take your breath away

The things that wake you up in the middle of the night in sweats…

A voice in your head will express its concerns for you

It will tell you it cannot be done

It will remind you of all the times you have failed before

Of all the times you've let yourself down

It won't see the stars behind your eyes

It won't know about the furnace deep inside

Your courage will remind it of all the times you have not succeeded

Of all the times you have let others down

It will project onto you

What is and isn't true

Not because it doesn't care...

Not because no love is there...

But to protect you from the hurt

Of broken memories

But behind the cuts

Is a plead

For you to dig deep

To self source the spring of hope

Within yourself, for yourself

So pull the pieces of yourself together

Even when there is doubt

Even when the embers burn

Even when you're buried under

Even when the road is covered in tar

Because you are the alchemist

And you always lead the way

Because there is no other way.

So whatever you do

Please

Please, don't ever give up on you.

25

IT'S CALLED MAGIC

What does the potion of a witch look like?

It's a shift in the air. A movement of heaviness sweeping through. The shudder of an icy cold touch, replaced by the warmth of sunlight reaching in.

It's a clay figurine molded into the likeness of a snake.

Metamorphic of a journey of transformation.

I didn't grow up thinking that I'd end up giving lap dances to married men for twenty bucks a pop as a teenager. Taking my clothes off in dimly lit clubs thick with cigarette smoke.

The golden handcuffs, that's what the girls called it. Once you're in it's impossible to get out.

Success felt like it never would be mine.

I didn't believe in the impossible.

I certainly didn't believe in the magic of money.

My world felt burned to flames.

Ashes everywhere I looked.

Until one night, a dragon came to visit me.

"Here's to the success of your new venture!" Chalices filled with warm cacao raised to the window, outside a fat full moon hangs low in the sky.

I'm at Jake's house. He no longer triggers me. Instead, his ease with cash inspires me.

We take turns going around the small circle of four, each sharing our intentions and sealing it with a celebratory cheer of our potions.

There's a lot for me to celebrate.

My first book is complete and I've just completed a workshop on magic that was deeply aligned, bringing in over $70,000 in revenues in a single month. What's more, another unexpected five figures hit my account from the sale of my remaining shares of my last company.

All my outstanding debts have been paid and I'm back in surplus.

None of it makes sense. I know.

Try to explain such things to those who see the world through the veil of Maya, it never will.

"Your turn," Jake encourages me.

I take a deep breath; I know what I want.

I close my eyes and cross into an astral plane, a spider that pulls at the strings of time.

There, I encounter the younger version of myself. Dark circles under her eyes, stressed and hopeless.

She's trying to convince a customer to give her money. Just one song, she promises.

It takes a moment for her to see me. Eyes darting in confusion.

You were the dragon all along, I tell her, and then I am gone.

She thought it was the alcohol. She was not ready to understand any more. But in the glimmer of a blue scale, she found the courage to move her life forward.

And she came to believe in the impossible.

I used to believe that money was some-thing separate from love.

Now, I understand money is an expression of love itself.

Forged in the greatest cauldron of all, the one within ourselves.

And where is your magic now?

It never left.

EXERCISE: INVITING THE DRAGON

When I hosted my first Money Magic workshop in 2022, I didn't expect the dragon to take the forefront of the stage.

Yet this was what resonated most with everyone.

Within a matter of days, participants began reporting seeing dragons everywhere, sharing pictures of it inside the private group.

Appearing on the carpets of libraries, sculptures of buildings, on clothing and even in random conversations.

Take this time to set the intention to be shown your dragon.

Then keep your eyes peeled. It will appear, I promise you.

Often, manifested in strange and unusual ways.

When it does, celebrate it as proof that your dragon has your back, that it wishes to serve you, that it has never truly left you.

If you feel inspired to do so, share pictures of your dragon inside the free Facebook group Flow Protocols or on Instagram by tagging me @cathowell—I would love nothing more than to celebrate your dragon with you.

And remember, the mind that can see dragons, is the same one capable of creating wealth.

AFTERWORD

A month after setting our intentions under the full moon I would go on to teach a workshop, sharing the dragon with the world, and bring in an additional six figures in revenues.

I wish I could tell you that my whole life has been a fairytale since then but that would lead you astray.

As more money came pouring in, my desires for even more freedom expanded. I engaged the divine feminine through rituals, compelling forth a new level of receiving I had not experienced before. I connected deeply with the desire to publish more books.

I asked my dragon for freedom and my dragon asked me to break away from all those things that came to make me feel trapped.

However, my actions did not reflect this big new juicy desire.

I still acted, spoke and behaved like the version of myself existing at the level before. I forced myself into a business model that wasn't made for me. I wasn't writing. I wasn't leading the way with the freedom I sought.

And so chaos arose.

Gee and I would go on to break up and get back together many times over.

The flames made me forgetful. I shunned my dragon, turned my back to it.

I'm only human.

Even though I live and breathe these concepts, I sometimes forget. It's often much easier to mentor and advise others than it is yourself.

But through the flames and chaos, I found my hand once more. Money Magic, the book, was born and I found the courage to realign how I ran my business.

And so goes the making of a myth. The protagonist desires for something, and it is in facing seemingly insurmountable obstacles, that they establish themselves as the professional hero of their own tale.

Happily ever after is an interim stop until new desires spring forth.

Each level requires the intentional marriage of intention and action.

Each level requires us to trust in unknowns.

Each level requires us to remember: that the mind that imagines a dragon, is the one that compels forth its treasures.

Be gentle and kind to yourself through the process. And forgive yourself for what has come before.

Today is a new day.

On the astral plane, your dragon awaits.

ENDNOTES

1. Speaker–listener neural coupling underlies successful communication, Greg J. Stephens, Lauren J. Silbert, Uri Hasson, 2010

2. The 'myth' of language history: Grammar changes faster than vocabulary, Max Planck Institute for the Science of Human History, 2017

3. The History of Money, Jack Weatherford, Victor Bevine, 2010

4. Exploring the Mesopotamina Trade: Types, Organisation, and Expansion. PalArch's Journal of Archeology of Egypt/ Egyptology, Arslan Butt, Ph. , Pakeeza Tabassum, Ph. , Farhat Saeed Imran, 2023

5. Cooperation in large-scale human societies—What, if anything, makes it unique, and how did it evolve? Simon T. Powers, Carel P. van Schaik, Laurent Lehmann, 2021

6. How Customers Think: Essential Insights into the Mind of the Market, Gerald Zaltman, 2003

7. Olfactory Influences on Mood and Autonomic, Endocrine, and Immune Function, Janice K. Kiecolt-Glaser, Jennifer E. Graham, William B. Malarkey, Kyle Porter, Stanley Lemeshow, and Ronald Glaser, Psychoneuroendocrinology. 2008

8. An Instinct for Dragons, Dr David E. Jones, 2002

9. The Griffin and the Dinosaur: How Adrienne Mayor Discovered a Fascinating Link Between Myth and Science, 2014, Marc Aronson

10. Mental Life and medical Illness: A Study of General Practice Patients, Michael Gruis, 2005

11. Posse, M., & Hallstrom, T. (1998. Alexithymia, personality,
characteristics, and somatization tendency in different physical diseases. European Journal of Psychiatry

12. Antall, G., & Kresevic, D. (2004. The use of guided imagery to manage pain in an elderly orthopaedic population. Orthopaedic Nursing

13. Diespecker, D (1990. Applied imagery. The Australian Journal of Clinical Hypnotherapy and Hypnosis

14. Functional near-infrared spectroscopy assessment of reward perception based on visual self-expression: Coloring, doodling, and free drawing. Girija Kaimal, Hasan Ayaz, Joanna Herres, Rebekka Dieterich-Hartwell, Bindal Makwana, Donna H. Kaiser, Jennifer A. Nasser. 2017

15. What is "the unconscious," and where is it located in the brain? A neuropsychoanalytic perspective. Department of Psychology, University of Cape Town, Mark Solms

16. Gnosis: An Esoteric Tradition of Mystical Visions and Unions, Dan Merkur, State of University New York Press, 1993

17. A Prehistoric Mural in Spain Depicting Neurotropic Psilocybe Mushrooms? Economic Botany, Brian P. Akers, Juan Francisco Ruiz, Alan Piper and Carl A. P. Ruck, 2011

18. The Immortality Key: The Secret Religion With No Name, Brian Muraresku, 2020

RESOURCES

You can access a free money dragon meditation on Youtube to support your journey by searching for 'Command a Blue Money Dragon' on my Youtube channel.

For more discussions on money, flow and the red light/green light system be sure to check out the Flow Protocols podcast.

If you enjoyed this book it would mean the world to me if you could leave a review on Amazon (or send me an email at support@theflowprotocols.com, this always makes my day).

Thanks again for reading and trusting me through this journey.

AKNOWLEDGMENTS

All myth is created within the tapestry of our relationships and this book is no different.

Thank you to Gee and my children for allowing me to share intimate parts of our story together and for reflecting back to me those parts of myself that I warred with.

To my community who rallied around me when I confessed to my magical practice and accepted me as I am. I am truly grateful for your ongoing support and this book would not exist without your enthusiasm and involvement in the first Money Magic workshop I held.

And to my dragon, thank you for always being there for me. I know I've not always been kind towards you, I know I sometimes forget you, but your loyalty and devotion inspires me forward.

ABOUT THE AUTHOR

Cat Howell is a Canadian author (see that, I get to call myself an author woo hoo!) and entrepreneur who has called NZ home for the last twenty years. You can check out more of her work at cathowell.com or connect with her on Instagram @cathowell .

ALSO AVAILABLE BY THE AUTHOR

Magic Source Codes

Abracadabra - "I create as I speak"

The world of alchemy is shrouded in stigma and fear, but for those who dare open their hearts awaits an empowering practice of self discovery.

Explore what new research reveals about the infamous witch hunts, how our ancestors amplified intentions, and the science behind magic.

Shared as an intimate memoir, Magic Source Codes is a compelling exploration and practical guide to the creative capacities of the human mind and the magical methods used to enhance wellbeing.

"A well written, intimate memoir that explains how the author used practical magical techniques (we're talking about real magick, not illusory magic) to resolve a serious case of depression. Highly recommended for those who are interested in the practical application of magical methods to improve their lives." - Dr Dean Radin, Author, Real Magic

Printed in Great Britain
by Amazon

37280701R00111